To Lose, But Not Fail

by William Gannon

Acknowledgments

Many thanks to those who made this book possible, including most of all, Renee Nalbandian Morehouse. Without Renee this book would still be bouncing around my head. Also to my cousin, Cindi D. Pietrzyk for editing the book for me.

Foreword

by Ron Garney

I've often thought if I could time travel, one of the places I would go would be to the summer of 1985. My good friend Drew and I were picking up our friend Peter and his fiancée, whom we everyone called Babe, at her mom's house so we could attend a screening of *Rocky IV*. This was the first time I met Babe's younger brother Billy, a spry, witty, fourteen-year-old boy who seemed to target me as sort of an older brother. I remember him asking me to make muscles for him so he could hang off my arm, only to have him remark how my arms, although muscular, needed to be more cut, triggering the laughter of everyone around us, including myself (I was a weightlifter at the time!). Bill tagged along with us to the movie, and sat next to me in the theatre. I noticed how we both indulged in the joy of punching the backs of the seats in the theatre as if they were heavy bags as Rocky took on his nemesis Drago.

I didn't see Billy again after that for four or five years—he was going through the normal years of his adolescence, although I had been told of some of the unfortunate events that shaped the rest of his life. As I was transitioning from a bartending job to Marvel entertainment, a career that has spanned my last two decades, I had a short-lived career as an athletic director for a local vacationing /corporate party resort in the area named "Holiday Hill." It was there I saw Bill again, but this time he was now a much larger young man, and was attending his senior high school graduation party. We eyeballed each other with the look of recognition as he was playing watermelon football in the resort pool. "I know you!" he finally said. "I know you, too!" I replied. We both had big grins from ear to ear. It took all of a few seconds for us to pick up where we left off like we had known each other forever. I recall Bill making some smart remark about my hair, and I "helped" him by sneaking him fresh eggs in the egg toss competition. With each successive one he and his partner dropped, I commented on their lack of athleticism.

3

This sort of funny, stone-busting repartee has been the trademark of my relationship with Bill for the past many years, and truthfully ever since that summer afternoon in 1985. But more than anything, what strikes me about our friendship is the ease and comfort with which it started, as if the established brotherly bond had been there forever. Bill and I never hesitated to engage each other—on the volleyball court at his brother-in-law's or in a wrestling match in his mom's pool. I had to have eyes in the back of my head to avoid Bill shoving me in! The same could be said for his beautiful wife Agnes. Every time I saw her, she joined right in the ceremony that would ensue between Bill and I. I'd always be reassured she was the perfect fit for him.

So, if I were a time traveler, I would go back to 1985 and tell Bill and his friends to not get in that car that fateful night. I would try and warn him about the other painful events that he describes so vividly and honestly in this book. That's arrogant of me of course, to think I could challenge fate's plan for Bill. It's hard not to question that plan, though. I've witnessed tragedy after tragedy that has befallen him (and other members of his family)—the accident in high school and the death of his two best friends, the loss of his child, the loss of his parents, and the horrible loss of the mother of his children and love of his life, Agnes. It's almost as if the strength of Bill's soul was something to be tested over and over again, and the only conclusion that could possibly make any sense is that it *has* to be for a reason no one can understand.

If it was a question of Bill's faith, or a question of his heart, or his core, I suggest it's a waste of time. Bill's resolve through his personal tragedies has proven over and over again that the strength of his character is unmatched. His exceptional devotion to his three amazing children and his unwavering ability to bounce back and still manage to be positive through everything he and his family has endured is inspirational. It is a testament to what kind of man he is.

From that boy hanging off my arm looking up to me, Bill has grown into a man whom I admire, a man from whom most men can learn. I'm honored to be in his life and to have him consider me one of his closest friends, as I consider him one of mine. I would love to be selfish and say all of this was unique to me in my relationship with Bill, but it's not gone unnoticed to everyone around that Bill has a unique way of making everyone feel at ease and connected with him. A truly kind and gifted soul resides there.

I just wish he'd get a new haircut.

—Ron Garney

Bill Gannon (left) and Ron Garney (right) at Rustic Oak

Introduction

When was the last time you enjoyed a star-filled sky, a perfect sunset on the beach, and the foliage on a brisk fall day? Are you too busy and just don't have the time to stop and, as they say, smell the roses? Take it from me, we may not be able to control the world around us, but we *can* control the one inside us. Is it bad to be a little selfish? To take a little time for ourselves? In this hustle-and-bustle world, we schedule ourselves right up to the moment our heads hit the pillow. Life is short, so why do we overload our schedules to get the most out of life, and then end up missing the most important parts?

I know you've heard others say it before, but I'm going to say it again. When I was growing up, things were slower; life seemed simpler. People were definitely more respectful to each other. Where did that world go?

Do you ever stop and think of what you are thankful for? Do you work hard and buy the things you want for yourself or to impress others?

My life and the way I see things changed due to specific events in my life—some happy, some tragic. I don't know if my relating my experiences will help you with any of your struggles or maybe give you a different outlook on life, but, if anything, reading this book will give you a few minutes to yourself.

Part One: The Accident

January 20, 1989 my father asked me to stay home, but not taking his advice changed the direction of my life. What was supposed to be a night out with two friends turned into a nightmare. I remember that Friday night as if it were yesterday. The decision to go out is one that I have never regretted. It was my choice, right or wrong. It was my choice and is something with which I have had to live and accept. It was just strange to me that my father asked me to stay home. I never drank or did drugs in high school. My sights were set on becoming a professional quarterback. When I was growing up, my father never pushed me into sports, but I guess I was destined to follow in his footsteps. My father could play any sport and played them all well. Drafted out of high school by the Pittsburg Pirates and then moving on to play for the Baltimore Orioles, he made a name for himself, and set a high bar for me. I remember coaches wanting me on their teams simply because I was "Bull" Gannon's son.

My friends, Marc Izzo and Matt Escoto were always happy, always joking around, and living every day to the fullest. They were the last two you would have to worry about when going out. They were two guys who always offered their support. Our friendship formed in seventh grade, and in the five years we knew each other I never saw either one of them without a smile on their faces—except for the night of January 20, 1989—a night that took Marc's life and changed both Matt and me for the rest of our lives.

The night started like most for a group of teens. We went to see a movie after a day of exams. There were no ominous danger signs, no black cats, and no dark clouds passing in front of the moon, no hairs standing on the backs of our necks. To this day, I still can't remember what movie we saw. I do remember Jen Gargiulo, a girl with whom we were friends, was seeing the same film. We all sat together. After the film we made plans to meet up with Jen and her friends at my Grandmother Lunney's house. From there, we all decided to go to the local arcade.

At the arcade, we played a baseball game for about a half hour. It was about 10:00 p.m. Marc needed to be home in a half hour, so we headed out. Unfortunately, we needed gas, so we stopped at a Food Bag. Matt and I went inside while Marc put gas in the car. When we exited the store we noticed Marc speaking with two girls. The girls had followed us from the arcade to the gas station. Matt and I joined in on the conversation with the girls for a few minutes. The girls asked us to go to a party in Meriden with them. The driver of the vehicle then unzipped her pocketbook and showed me a bottle of 100-proof Smirnoff vodka. They continued to ask us if we would go with them, but Marc reminded us about the time and told them we had to get home.

We all proceeded to the car and got in, the only difference was this time I noticed Marc putting on his seatbelt. I was in and out of his car seven or eight times that day and no one had put on a seatbelt. Now moments before the accident, it seemed second nature to do so. I can't tell you how many people have told me that I had an angel looking over my shoulder that night. I won't argue with that.

We headed south on Route 5, listening to Billy Joel's "Piano Man." To this day every time I hear that song I think of my two friends. I broke into my pack of grape Hubba Bubba Bubblegum and Matt immediately leaned between the two front seats asking for a piece. When I turned to hand him the gum, I remember seeing Matt's eyes widen and hearing him yell. The next thing I remember was waking up and hearing Matt's screams from the back seat. The screams that leave no doubt on what our situation was. My vision was very cloudy, but I didn't feel any pain at this point. I remembered glass falling into my lap as I touched my face. The car's atmosphere had changed. Little did we know that our lives were as shattered as the windshield.

Only twenty minutes had passed, but it could have been ten seconds, I had no clue. I kept asking Matt if he was all right, but he just continued to scream. I couldn't even imagine what he was going through in that back seat. My body was in shock and I had yet to feel any pain. I didn't realize how severe the situation was.

I had hit my head and one of my eyes was completely swollen shut. Even though my head was fuzzy, and my vision blurred, I'll never forget the last image I had of Marc. We had been best friends since seventh grade, and this was the first time I'd seen his face without a smile. My chest felt empty, I got that lump in my throat, as I reached over to feel his pulse. I couldn't tell if it was my pulse or his? In my heart, I knew I had lost my friend. The things that rush through your mind in seconds that feel like hours are amazing. I just wanted to wake up because this wasn't supposed to happen to us. The situation grew grim, and I began to question my own mortality. They say in extreme circumstances a person can gather great strength from adrenaline. I tried three times to free myself from the dashboard with no success. I felt so helpless knowing they needed my help and I had nothing to offer. Matt's screams grew louder and more frequent. As bad as it was to hear him in pain, at least I knew he was still alive. It was as if my hearing was heightened at this moment. As I struggled to get to my friends, I thought I was going to die. Then I remembered the best moments I had with the people I loved. Each thought seemed to give me that strength, that edge. I got this amazing burst of mental energy, countering the lack of physical strength. My will to live kicked into overdrive. I wasn't ready to die. I remember thinking to myself: *I want to leave something behind. I wanted to be a father.*

Moments later, a fireman knocked on my window. After a few quick questions, he told me I was in better shape than my friends and that they needed to get them out first. As I looked over at the now empty driver's seat, it just didn't register to me that I would never see my best friend alive again. After freeing Matt from the back seat, they began to extract me from the car. I remember the rescue crew pulling me out, and when my left heel hit the ground, only a six-inch drop to the ground, it was like being hit by a bolt of lightning. The pain was so intense; it sent shockwaves through my entire body. Immediately they placed me on the board and secured my neck. The pain in my leg was like nothing I had felt before. I focused on the cold air to try and relieve some of the pain, but it didn't work. Despite my best efforts, I still felt the sharp and intense pain. I was being loaded into the ambulance, when an officer asked me for some information. He needed Marc's and Matt's home addresses. Although I had been to both houses many times, I never knew the exact addresses. I did, however, give him their phone numbers and directions to their houses. Shock had set in physically, but there's no mental shock, nothing, really, to dull that pain. When the ambulance doors closed, I couldn't help but think of what was left in that car.

I tolerated the physical pain during the ambulance ride to the hospital. But, I remember thinking, *Why us, why us?* This wasn't supposed to happen to us. Marc and Matt were good kids, good students. They had their whole lives already mapped out. They wanted to be pilots. And now, who knew where the road was going to lead? At this point I was scared and confused. Scared because I realized I did not have any control or movement of my left leg. No matter how much or how many ways I tried to move it, there was nothing. I was afraid to tell the paramedic. I didn't want to lose my leg. I thought if I could just buy some time, maybe some feeling would come back. It was that never-say-die attitude I must have developed from my years of sports.

I remember arriving at a hospital in Meriden. I know I was in dire need of treatment, but I also knew I wouldn't get it at this hospital. It seemed like a lot of time had passed and I was wondering where my family was. I thought they would have been there by now. I found out later from my sisters that my father had a hard time accepting the news, and at first couldn't bring himself to go to the hospital. The first people I saw actually were my football coach and Charlie Dugan. A friend's sister had noticed me being wheeled into the hospital and had called her father. Charlie Dugan's son Chucky played football with me. Mr. Dugan wanted the best for all us kids: he was that type of guy. They wanted to know if there was anything they could do for me. I told them, "I'm sure they're on their way, but could you get in touch with my family?" When my coach left, I lay there thinking of how I had let so many people down.

The doctor from the Meriden-Wallingford hospital told me I was in serious condition, so they needed to get me into surgery immediately. I couldn't accept that diagnosis without him even taking a single x-ray. I was in bad shape, but not that bad. I told the doctor that I was seventeen and not dying, so he needed my parents' consent. I just wanted to go home, but there was no going back. I knew I had to face the truth that was now in front of me. Not long after the doctors left, my family arrived. I could see the pain on my parents' faces even though my right eye was swollen shut, and vision in my left eye wasn't that great, either. Some situations don't need words.

As I lay on that stretcher, my father's voice telling me not to go out echoed in my head. I felt as if I ruined everything. All the camps, equipment, and training—was it all for nothing? My mother kissed me on the forehead and asked how I was. I told her I was fine. That's when she told me that the doctors wanted to amputate my leg. I couldn't imagine life without my leg. I remembered my father's words that you can lie to anyone, but you can't lie to yourself. This was my moment of truth. I knew feeling bad for myself wasn't going to help my leg get any better, so I had a major gut check and focused on what was next. This was one of those things that wouldn't just play itself out.

They decided to move me to Yale New Haven Hospital. My sister Maureen, who had arrived with my parents, is a nurse and took the ambulance ride with me. In the ambulance, I asked her how bad my leg was. Her hesitation spoke volumes. I had twenty minutes before we would reach the hospital. I refused to believe that tomorrow I would be without a leg, the competitive side of me was breaking through, and I began to focus on my toes. I was looking for any sort of sign, any movement. I was praying for a tingle, a pins-and-needles sensation, but there was nothing. I would pinch my thigh to see if I could feel anything, I couldn't. I didn't feel anything but the radiating pain by my pelvis. With time against me, I had no choice but to dig deeper. I had a small window to make something positive happen. About two minutes before we reached the hospital, I moved my second toe.

Thinking that wouldn't be enough, I focused on my other toes. When the doors opened, I could move three out of five toes. I thought I was ready to take on the world. I didn't realize I had only won a battle; the war loomed large ahead of me.

As soon as I was pushed through the doors, a medical team swarmed me. They started a battery of tests from blood work to x-rays to cat-scans. It's a strange feeling to welcome a surgery, but I did. The hours of pre-op testing plays games with your mind. Everything is a big question mark and only God knows the outcome. All the time had passed and nobody had any answers for me. At this point I was wishing for tomorrow, I didn't think I was going to die, but I wanted control of the situation. I remember saying a quick prayer before they put the mask on my face to knock me out. It's funny how quick we turn to God when things go bad. I was out; the surgery was about to start. My life, my leg, and all my other problems were in his hands.

I remember waking up in the I.C.U. My left leg was in traction and there was a tube coming out of my chest under my right arm to re-inflate my collapsed lung. It was then that I found out the extent of my injuries. My pelvic girdle was fractured in eight places; I had seven broken ribs, a concussion, a bruised heart, and multiple contusions and lacerations. The first thing I did was look at my hip to see how big my scar was. It was only about six inches long, and I thought, *Wow, technology rules.* Then I began to wonder if things were better than they thought; after all, I only had a six-inch scar, and that doctor in Meriden wanted to take my leg off.

The nurse in my unit asked if there was anything I needed. I wanted to see someone from my family. When my parents entered the room, the feeling that I had let them down came flooding back. I know they just wanted me to be okay, but I also knew I had disappointed them. My parents asked me if there was anything they could do for me. I told them I wanted a private hospital room, so I could just have control of something. Little did they know how much that meant to me. They came through on the room, but the rest was up to me. A single room gave me the opportunity to focus without any distractions. I received very limited information on Marc and Matt. Everyone was trying to protect me, shelter me for that moment.

The next two weeks were filled with x-rays, blood work three times a day, shots, pills, but no therapy. I didn't understand why until they started the pre-op tests again. I was confused to say the least. *Why do they need to go back in?* I thought. That's when I found out that the first surgery had only been to stabilize things and remove the bone fragments. I felt defeated, as if I couldn't get that first grip to start my climb. My mother somehow must have sensed this. She was there when the weight of everything got too heavy for my shoulders. She first started to joke. Then when that didn't work, she kissed my head and hugged me as I vented. That moment catapulted my spirit more than she'll ever know. She provided me with that solid foundation I needed for the months ahead.

Hospital stays are never fun, bad food, limited channels and the same four walls. There is a lot of time to think. It brought me back to my first hospital stay. My first five years of life were, for the most part, normal. I was the baby and had four older sisters. There was always a battle for a bathroom or a TV. My mother was a homemaker and always there for us; my father was an ultimate provider. My mom and dad both worked hard. Mom stayed home and dealt with us kids, and Dad held down two jobs outside the house. He would leave the house at eight in the morning, come back for dinner a little after five, then by six he would be out the door to his cleaning company. One of my father's quotes I heard often was, "You do what you gotta do."

William "Bull" Gannon

While my childhood was uneventful for the most part, my sisters and I got into our share of trouble. One of my first and most vivid memories is a painful one. One weekend morning, my sister Mo (fifteen at the time), was making bacon in the kitchen. My youngest sister, Jessica (seven at the time), was chasing me. Dad was reading the newspaper, and told me to stop running. Of course, I didn't listen, as most five-year-olds don't, and seconds later I was running through the kitchen, not looking where I was going. Bam! I ran right into Mo, who was pouring the hot bacon grease into the sink. The grease spilled onto my chest and under my chin like slow motion. The sound of my skin crackling from the grease was almost as bad as the pain itself. I remember my father picking me up and throwing me on the couch, and my mother running in with a bag of ice, which she gently placed on my chest.

The emotion on my family's faces was a telltale sign of how bad the situation was, even for a five year old.

The next thing I recall is being in the car and on my way to the hospital, which was just up the street. I was later told that my parents had called 911, but were told that it would be quicker if they drove me themselves. As soon as we got there my dad carried me into the hospital where a group of doctors and nurses were waiting. Everything was chaos, but they stabilized me.

I was then moved to Yale New Haven Hospital, where they performed a skin graft from my left thigh. I was in the hospital for about five weeks. As a kid, five weeks felt like five months. The majority of the time, my hands had to be strapped to the bed rails so I couldn't touch my chest.

At this age I was into dinosaurs. My father bought me every dinosaur I could think of. I remember one doctor who would come into my room often and ask, "Did you just see that T-Rex go by the window?" Even at my young age, I could see how many people wanted to make me feel better. That care helped in my recovery, but also showed me what love and heart can achieve.

While I don't remember all the details about my stay in the hospital, I do remember this one boy who had cancer. He would come into my room every day to play. Being five, I didn't know about cancer. To me, he was just a boy with a baldhead.

It's funny how we don't always see the big picture. There were many times when I would have traded places with my friend. Here I was, restrained to a bed and had no mobility between rooms. Granted I was five years old, but I wasn't able to see my friend had the greater obstacle in front of him. I was living in a temporary mindset, not seeing the big picture.

One day, when my new friend and I were in my room playing, my father walked in with a King Kong doll that I wanted. The only problem was my friend wanted it as much as I did. I was surprised when my dad gave the toy to my friend instead of me. I remember my friend being so excited and running back to his room with his new toy. My father smiled and asked how I was doing. I told him I wanted that King Kong doll. But, Dad patiently explained to me that I only *wanted* the doll, but that little boy *needed* it. He explained to me that this boy had a lot more to overcome than I did. Then my father promised to buy me another King Kong, but I told him I didn't want one. That moment, that important lesson, was imprinted in my memory.

We all left that experience with something. It turned out to be a win, win for all of us. At the tender age of five, I realized that even though it seemed like I was there forever, I would get to go home, but other kids wouldn't. My father was right; they did have more to overcome.

After my stay in the hospital, my life went almost back to normal. Except for applying cocoa butter to my chest and having to wear a t-shirt to keep the sun off the wound, I was good to go! Although, having to wear a shirt all the time made me a little self-conscious. Having to always cover my scar made me feel as if I had something to hide.

In fifth grade, got my next test of physical pain. I was walking down the stairs when I stepped on a needle. That, by itself, didn't hurt, but what I didn't know was that a piece of the needle had broken off. It was about a week or so before I felt any pain and realized something was wrong. We went to the doctor and they took x-rays of my foot, which showed remains of the needle beginning to travel up my blood stream; I was going to need surgery. Not major surgery, but it would require a stay in the hospital. I always refer to that surgery as a walk in the park.

Back to the here and now, you see, the past may have prepared me a little better for this, and I needed to use everything I could to my advantage. I wasn't afraid of the second surgery after the accident. I just wanted to fix what needed to be fixed and move on to the next challenge. There was a resident doctor who would sit with me every night just to answer any questions I had. He kept telling me that I had come a long way from that first night. He reminded me how well I was doing, and how this next surgery would bring me that much closer to returning home. He was one of many who kept on me about reaching my goals. There were many nights when I would question what everyone saw in me?

The ten-hour surgery was a success; however the night in I.C.U. was less than wonderful. Those of you who have been in this situation can understand; and for those who haven't, I hope you never will. You see after any long procedure, your throat gets as dry as a desert, but you are only allowed to have a cup of ice chips. I ate as much ice as I could, as fast as I could—and then paid the price. Within five minutes of eating that ice, I began violently throwing up. I never liked vomiting, but with seven broken ribs, I liked it even less. Everyone, including me, assumed I was throwing up because of the ice chips, but about eight hours later they found out it was because I had an allergic reaction to the pain medication Demerol. It was a long night without any pain medicine or ice chips. The only thing I had to look forward to was returning to my room.

I remember them hooking me up to this leg machine that helps with your range of motion and flexibility. The actual placement of my leg on the machine didn't hurt, but when they started the machine, the pain was so intense that I began to scream and twist the pull-up bar. I twisted the bar so many times around with such force, that I bent a few of the links. My mother begged the nurse to shut it off. After about three minutes, she did. The nurse waited for the attending doctor to assess the situation. The doctor concluded that I was allergic to the medication, and I didn't have any painkillers in my system to start therapy.

This was the most pain that I had been in since the night of the accident, but it wasn't only my physical pain with which I was dealing.

I was given the news that Marc never made it. Marc was so young and had so much going for him. He had the ability to talk to anyone. It was hard for me to comprehend that someone so full of life and heart could leave us so soon. It took a good six to eight months to get that last image of him out of my head and remember the always-happy Marc. It was hard to believe all I had left were memories. Even to this day, there's that pause before you can find the words to describe such an amazing person.

Matt was in Hartford Hospital waging his own battle with injuries. He became very close to God after the accident. That transition always amazed me. We talked to each other on the phone about how boring the hospital was and what we would do after we got out. Those thoughts gave me hope and took my mind to a place outside the walls of that room. I remember him telling me he didn't remember anything that happened that night. Some nights I would think how lucky he was not to have it running constantly through his mind. At this point, he never even questioned me about the accident.

I kept thinking this was our fate. My friend Joe Kurcaba was going to join us, but didn't. Joe was born with a clef palate, which made me realize all people were not created equal, but that life sends us down separate paths, it challenges us all in different ways. He was one to always hold his head high, let the comments and teasing go in one ear and out the other. I believe God intertwines certain people in our lives to help us on our journey, maybe even prepare us for future events. Joe, his nickname Chopper, had a big impact on my life.

Chop wasn't dealt the best hand, but he played and continues to stay in the game of life. He is a great example for me to learn by, and a better friend.

I continued to be positive, but recovery was long and difficult. However, it is through these trials that some of life's best lessons are learned. The next day I received one of those lessons. My therapist, Rick, wheeled me into the therapy room. I asked him where we were going to begin. He placed me in the center of the room and began pointing out patients. He first pointed out a man in a wheelchair, and said, "That man is twenty-two, a quadriplegic, he'll never walk again." Then he pointed out a man who was paraplegic, and said, "Only a miracle will allow him to walk again." Rick then turned my attention to a twenty-year-old man lying in a therapy bed. He asked, "See that man there? He's dying of AIDS; he'll be dead in six months."

As I digested this information, Rick continued, "Five minutes ago you probably thought your injuries were pretty bad, that you were the worst in the world, but you're not!"

He was right. I thought I was scraping the bottom of the barrel. It's funny how our minds play tricks on us. I was going back and forth emotionally. On one hand I was happy to be alive, but on the other hand I was upset that I had worked so hard at football, and now I might never play again. It was odd to me that words, not medicine or therapy, propelled me to get back on my feet.

I returned to my room without moving a muscle and had an entire twenty-four hours to think about Rick's lesson. This is where my years of sports came into play. I didn't know where the road would lead me, but I wasn't going down without a fight. I had started for two years on the varsity football team that went 19 to 1. We ended up winning the last game on Thanksgiving Day. I didn't know how to go down without a fight.

My dreams still felt obtainable. I didn't end on my terms and I worked way to hard to just give in. The older I got, the more my father recognized my talent. He would add his two cents, not caring about mistakes as long as I could think about them and correct them.

I had decided to make it my mission to save my parents some money and try for a scholarship for college, so now I had four years to make an impression on college scouts. About two weeks after I finished eighth grade, I went to the Joe Namath Football Camp. I remember being late the first day. We were supposed to be there at 8:00 a.m. to get our playbooks and review them. My father dropped me off at 8:45 a.m. I didn't even have anyone there to help me with my equipment. When I got out on the field, one of the coaches wanted me to take the offense's reigns. He had me run eight plays, and I messed up eight times. To make it worse, Joe Namath was there watching, and he let me know he knew I was messing up. What a way to begin! I started to think that maybe football wasn't for me; I was struggling mentally and physically.

We had an hour and a half break for lunch. There were a bunch of kids playing basketball in the gym, so I decided to join them. I was the youngest kid out there. Everyone else was a junior or senior in high school. They were all bigger and much slower than me. I was blowing by them as if they were standing still. I was hitting three pointers and throwing passes like a pro. I don't know if it was just one of those days or if it was just fate, but Joe Namath was watching again. He called me over to talk to me again. He asked, "Why can you look so good on a basketball court, but look so bad on the football field?"

I told him that I had played basketball for years, but had never played football. He couldn't understand why I didn't tell him that morning. I said I didn't want to make excuses; I just wanted to get better. Something I said must have made an impression because Joe took me under his wing, teaching me as much as I could take in. He showed me a lot of the tricks of the trade. That first day none of the other kids had wanted me to be on their team; two days later they all wanted me.

With Joe's help, my mechanics were completely different physically. He taught me to throw about sixty-five yards, how to throw to the receivers in different situations, and how to understand the different trajectories of the football. The experience from this one-week of camp was more than I would have received if I had played for years. Joe didn't have to help me out the way that he did, but he showed me that with a little help and hard work, that I could accomplish some great things in a short amount of time. He also showed me that no matter how famous I become I should always give back. The other thing that stuck in my mind was when Joe told me was that there had been ten guys in his college days who were just as good as he was, but he took advantage of his opportunity. He taught me a lot about life

I worked every day that summer to make me a better football player. On certain days I would throw anywhere from 500 to 1,000 balls a day. I would run, jump rope, and throw every day. I didn't want to just be the best in my school; I wanted to be the best ever. I knew I needed to learn the game, so I wanted to be sure that my physical shape wasn't an issue.

That summer went by so fast. Before I knew it, it was time for conditioning week. This was the week where we were required to be at the school for 5:00 p.m. We would spend two hours in the classrooms, before going outside to do the conditioning aspect of the training. Because I went to camp, I was the only freshman with a helmet. This was a problem with a few upperclassmen; I guess they didn't think I had paid my dues yet? Interestingly enough, it wasn't the kids who were the starters; it was the group of kids who had never really played who had the issues with me. As we started our ten-minute run around the football field, I started to get a lot of comments from these players. The idea of the run was to get around the field ten times in ten minutes. On my first night, I circled the field fourteen times in ten minutes, not to make an impression, but just to run by these players. I found out quickly that high school was a free for all; it was going to be another challenge that would make me who I am today. That old saying that talk is cheap; you find out how true that rings really fast. I found out I needed their respect if I was going to lead the team.

I knew I needed to be in better physical shape than most of these upperclassmen, but as we went into our first scrimmage, I was the one sitting on the bench. When my chance to play finally came, the last thing I wanted to do is mess up. Of course, that's exactly what happened: I went right as my team went left. It was only me and the defensive end, and thirty yards to the end zone. I scored, but that didn't stop the coach from tearing into me. Discipline and teamwork are definitely needed in a contact sport.

The first game of my freshman year I split time with another quarterback, but we got crushed. In the car on the ride home, I told my mother I thought I should go to the hospital. She said, "You'll be fine." I guess I was looking for some sympathy, but if my mother is not going to give me any, I should just throw in the towel right then and there. It did make me tougher, both physically and mentally. She was a football mom and knew when to praise me and when to push me. And, yes she was right.

I knew that good things come to those who wait; but I knew they also come to those who work hard. Every night before I went to bed, I said my prayers and then tried to control or gain control of my body. Negativity can spread like wildfire in a hospital, so you have to keep reinforcing a positive attitude. Rick never allowed me to quit; he constantly challenged me. Day after day, rep after rep, it was all about gaining ground.

But despite my best efforts, the doctors were still all over the board when it came to my recovery. Worst-case scenario said it would be two years before I could start walking again. Best-case scenario said one year. I said six months. I developed selective hearing and began to hear only what I wanted to hear. Take into consideration I was dealing with a hip injury, not damage to a major organ. The pain would have to take a backseat to my passion; at this point I was shooting for a full recovery. Every day was a personal challenge to get better. In my mind, I felt as if the doctors only saw an injury; they didn't see the person I was.

The accident received local media attention. Local newspapers quoted me as saying I would make it back to the playing field. This forced me to stay honest with my recovery. Most people must have thought I was crazy, but that didn't stop them from rallying behind me. I received letters from friends and former teachers, mayors from surrounding towns and Congressmen, even Connecticut senators. I had a lot of people in my corner, a lot of people who wanted me to succeed, and their encouragement kept me in the right frame of mind.

I wanted to win every game and I hated to lose, but no matter how much I gave, things weren't going my way. It's said a chain is only as good as its weakest link;

likewise a team is only as good as its weakest player. We lost 19 games in a row. We all knew we were improving with every passing week, but were we good enough to win against our cross-town rivals Lyman Hall?

Thanksgiving 1988 was a day of eye-opening proportions. I remember the car ride to school with my father. The only thing different was me, I remember thinking about just getting through the game. I was basically writing the contest off. I never thought the other team couldn't be beat, so where was my head? It was off having turkey after the game. I was thinking about the next season. As I exited the car, my father set the spark by saying, "Have one today". As I walked to the locker room, I thought of how hard he worked for our family. Trying to feed off of my father's words, I walked into the locker room. It wasn't as loud as it usually was. Yes, my friend Chucky didn't change his routine, he continued to head-butt the lockers to get fired up.

That Thanksgiving morning we were holding our own, but couldn't get the ball in the end zone. After being stopped on the goal line, I knew if we didn't score the next time we got the ball, we could lose faith in ourselves. Our team needed this; I wanted to set a tone for my teammates and the game on the next possession. We got the ball in our territory and gained a few yards on first down with a running play, and then with a pass interference call we were sitting on our own twenty-six-yard line, twenty-six yards later we were on the scoreboard. It's amazing to see how people react to a positive moment. Although we had been in striking distance before, we had that swagger about us. We got the ball back on the ensuing kick-off, and two plays later I ran sixty-five yards for another touchdown. Our stands finally had something to cheer about, and cheer they did. All the sudden, we were a different team.

Our next series, I threw for a touchdown, putting us up by three scores. The game seemed to be ours, but on our next series, I was hit solidly in the chest by a three-hundred-pound lineman, and it was hard to get up. Lyman Hall scored right before half time, but we were a different team now. I tried to hide how much I was hurting.

I remembered how bad it was to lose the prior year, and I didn't want that. There was only one half left, and I wanted to go out a winner. I put my pain on the back burner.

When the second half started, I knew the Lyman Hall defense would be coming for me, and they did. Things were different though. We were a team now and everybody was doing his best. It paid off and we got our win.

When I left that field that day I was the M.V.P., but only because twenty-two other guys decided we could win. Sometimes it only takes a little push, or one moment to spark momentum in the right direction. It is that moment you need to seize. Everyone has his day; it's just a matter of taking advantage of that time when it comes. While I didn't realize it at the time, the lessons I learned from sports, mostly football would help me deal with what I was about to face.

I wanted to beat the odds for them and for me, but most of all, I wanted to do it for my father. Every time he walked into my room I seemed to get a second wind. My father was never much of a complainer; he just did what he needed to do, whether that meant working two jobs to support his family or whatever. Now I needed to do what needed to be done, no excuses, no complaints.

When you want to get better, you can't afford to feel sorry for yourself. You have to tell yourself, *I can.* You have to become more than your aliment. It really is up to you. You can have all sorts of support surrounding you, but if you're not the one leading the charge, then most likely you're the one setting yourself up to fail. You control your own world and you are the one who can change it. You have to prepare for setbacks when you're reaching for a goal.

Marc's parents came to see me; they wanted to be the ones to tell me Marc had passed away. While I had seen Marc the night of the accident and knew in my heart that he was gone, hearing his parents say it made it real to me.

I know now the feeling of losing a child, and I can appreciate how Marc's parents felt about me. People aren't replaceable, certainly not Marc. When they told me, I couldn't cry, but I was heartbroken. I decided that the best way to honor Marc would be to live everyday to the fullest. Marc was going to be more than just a memory. I still, once in a while, think I should have done something different, I don't know if I broken down if that would have meant more to them? But I also know that Marc was my best friend, he knew how I felt. I still think about him often, and whenever too much time passes when I haven't thought about either Marc or Matt, I hear Billy Joel's "The Piano Man," and know they're watching over me.

This was my first real experience with loss. Talking with Marc's parents was my test on how to gauge emotions; I failed big time. I wanted to share stories of the good times Marc and I had together, but at the time I felt like it would hurt his parents. If I could go back, I would have talked their ears off. As hard as it may be when you lose someone, I don't think there's anything better than knowing that your loved one touched someone's life and made a difference.

On top of dealing with my injury and the loss of my friend, I also had to deal with the logistics of the accident. The police were interviewing me every other day; they would come in and ask questions that never seemed to make any sense. "Where do you go to school?" "What year are you in?" They never asked any important questions about the accident. It was only later that I found out why.

Sometimes it's about whom you know and not what you know. The girl who caused the accident had some hefty connections. I heard her grandfather sold the police cruisers to the department. Of all the information being gathered about what happened, I think my statement was the only one that held any truth about what happened that horrific night. Matt had no memories of the accident, so I felt I was the only one who could clear Marc's name.

Another issue that arose during my recovery was school. The length of my hospital stay would determine if I would have to repeat junior year. I was determined to make my stay as short as possible. My will to win was doing its job. When I started to slide in the wrong direction, my parents would visit or call and put wind back into my sails.

Once I started physical therapy in earnest, time went into lightning speed. I set lofty goals for myself. When I hit a problem, I changed my routine or worked through it. Everybody has their moments, their bad days. When these days came, I used them as rest days and that's how I looked at it. During all our lives, there comes a point where we feel like we're cracking. A little cracking is fine as long as you don't break. I began to cross bridges as they came. I put things into perspective. As far as issues with the car accident, truth was on my side. When it came to the doctors, I would change their expectations. My mind set was in such a positive place that hearing the negative didn't bother me. I needed to hear the negative so I could prove it wrong. There is no substitute for positive thinking, regardless of your situation it's better to go out fighting.

I had another friend, Chris Selvaggi. Chris would call and visit to keep my sprits high and really impacted my life. He and I continued to push each other with our workouts, always trying to get better every day. I could call him at 11:00 p.m. to do hills, and he'd run every one with me. Chris was exactly what I needed to keep me in the right frame of mind. Chris was 100 percent when it came to working out. His passion complemented mine. There were very few rest days with Chris. A guy like that only raises everyone's game.

Chris Selvaggi (40)

I had enough fight in my system; I just didn't have the nourishment. The hospital food was horrible. My parents would bring me breakfast, lunch, and dinner. My friend Jay would make me a steak dinner once a week. I thought I was gaining weight, until I saw myself in the mirror. I could see every bone in my back. My weight was one hundred and twenty six pounds, a far cry from the one hundred and eighty six pounds I had been when I arrived at the hospital. The workouts were intense, and were burning more calories than I thought. I started eating five times a day and drinking three to five milkshakes daily to try and put the weight back on.

As my recovery progressed, I remember Rick saying, "You're getting bigger and better, but it's too early to get satisfied with the results." He challenged me to challenge myself. I was both physically and physiologically stronger. After a little more then two months in the hospital, I was ready to go home. The doctors agreed.

On our last day of therapy together Rick told me, "It was my job to get you moving in the right direction, but how far you got was up to you." At the time I didn't understand how right he was. It's how we approach things that determine their outcome. Doctors, nurses, therapists, etc., can only provide you with a good foundation; the rest is up to you. Like Rick said, he only gave me direction, how and when I reached my goal was up to me. I thanked him for both his words and workouts; they were worth their weight in gold. He wished me the best of luck as we shook hands, he went on his way to his next patient and I waited to get released from my hospital stay.

It seemed to take forever to get the release papers signed. Then the car ride home lasted an eternity; we hit every red light from the hospital to home. But those little things didn't bother me anymore. My father always used to say, "No biggie." Until the accident, I didn't know what he meant. Now I did. We all get wrapped up in petty things that mean absolutely nothing. I used to think, and still do, about how lucky I was and am. I focus on the positive. Sitting at those red lights, I just thought, *Ten minutes from now, I'll be home eating Mom's pancakes.*

Soon enough, I was home. I stepped out of the car with crutches in my hands. The cold night air reminded me of the night of the accident. I shook off the horror and thought of what needed to be done. I kept saying, "I'm home."

My parents had fixed up the finished basement for me. It wasn't my room, but it was home. I didn't have to worry about any stairs, and it had everything I needed—a shower, TV, bed, and a phone. My bed was right under a corkboard with pictures and newspaper articles from the prior football season. It brought me back to the summer of my freshmen year; I went to the Jim Kelly Camp for football. One night

29

Buffalo Bills lineman Tony Brown asked if anyone wanted to jog with him. No one else accepted the offer, but I thought *why not?* I agreed to join him. We had only covered about a mile and a half when he noticed he had lost his keys. We were both looking for about ten minutes when all the other Buffalo Bill players came to help out. They all introduced themselves to me, but three of them really stood out—Jim Kelly, Andre Reed, and Craig Swoop. Another bunch of super stars that were down-to-earth guys who just wanted to give something back.

Throughout my time at camp, Jim picked up where Joe Namath had left off; he brought me to that next level. When I returned home from Jim's camp I was on the top of the world! I increased the intensity of my workouts; I wanted to be the best. I was in shape, but skinny. I was five feet eleven inches and only weighed one hundred and forty five pounds. And, I was still not experienced enough to win a starting position. My coach knew how hard I was working, but I needed to convince my teammates I was the best for the job. The quarterback is the leader on the field and being young meant I had to prove myself that much more. It was almost like I was living that year all over again. I had to get bigger, stronger and now more to prove then before.

There was also a picture of my friend Marc. I would lie in my bed and think about him. There were a lot of nights where sleep would not come. I would take a shot of Nyquil just to get to sleep. Some nights I felt as if I was being consumed by an image created by the night of the accident.

As hard as it was, I wouldn't let negative thoughts dictate my drive. I felt God had put me on a path, pointed me in this direction, and then left it in my hands on how or if I would reach my new destination. I knew there were no guarantees in life, but I never imagined that life could get so bad, so quick. At eighteen, you're at the threshold of adulthood. Here I was, seventeen, and somewhat confused. I could accept a lot of things, but at times I still asked, *Why?* I guess you could spend a lifetime wondering why something bad has happened to you, but not waste a moment or count your blessings when something goes right. The sooner you get past the "why" stage, the quicker you begin to recover.

Once I was home, I had two days to myself before I would take on a very physically and mentally challenging recovery. Before I started, I had something I needed to do. Because of the weeks in bed, my equilibrium was off. I need to regain my strength and balance if I wanted to walk for an extended amount of time.

While all this was going on, my Grandfather Gannon was also in the hospital and almost died. My family told me that he kept asking, "Where's Billy?" They kept him at bay for a while by telling him I was busy with football, but then a friend told him I had been in a car accident. He wanted to see me more than anything then. I didn't want to disappoint him, so with the help of my mother; we both made the trip.

The walk to his room with crutches wasn't easy, and there were many times where I thought I might pass out. When I finally made it to his room, the look on his face, with the tears streaming down his cheeks, was worth every painful step. I put up a good front; I didn't want him to see my pain. My Grandfather Gannon and I share a sense of humor, so it was easy to keep my mind off my ailments. I drew strength from him and my mom. Seeing my grandfather's smile and hearing his jokes showed me the pain could be harnessed, controlled. Love and laughter are powerful agents to have on your side. My grandfather could always find humor in a situation, or at least use it to defuse the issue.

Over the next two days, a lot of people came to visit. Every time someone left, I would think, *these people must think I'm crazy!* I was frail and yet I kept telling everyone I was going to reach this goal. It also amazed me to hear the stories that had circulated about me in my absence. I spent most of the time clearing the air. Tales ranged from me having a glass eye to me having AIDS. I learned quickly to not get involved with the stories. I decided I would write my own headlines. I was in control of my life. There were also wild stories circulating about the accident itself. Regardless of the truth, some people will throw their own spin on things. The way I saw it, there were two things that I could do—buy into all the crap or use it to motivate me. I think it's obvious which way I went.

Playing quarterback teaches you to take the good with the bad. I recalled my sophomore year, I was nervous the first night of varsity training and that affected my training. It took me almost twice as long to learn the plays. I went home that night upset with myself because I knew I could play with them, but I certainly wasn't showing my teammates that I had what it took. I called my Uncle Joe that night and he told me, "Everybody has those days—it didn't matter if you were a high school player or a Hall of Famer."

The next day at practice, I was a different person. I still made plenty of mistakes, but now when I made them I moved past them and did better the next time around. I took a little pressure off myself and enjoyed the game; that's what had been missing.

The night before the first game, my coach told me I would be starting. He let me know because he wanted me to relax and focus on the game. Sometimes things have one appearance, but in reality are the total opposite. At the game, we marched down the field eighty yards and scored on my first drive. I was three for three passing. I thought, *Wow my stats are going to be awesome.* Maybe it was luck, or at that moment we were up to the challenge, but during the next series, the bottom fell out. It took eight games to even score.

On game eight of the season, we were in East Haven and it was -4°F. It was the end of the third quarter and the score was 21 to 0. I was the only one on the field not wearing gloves, I could throw in all the elements, Uncle Joe had prepared me for that. I threw three touchdowns to send the game into overtime. The game was not to be ours, though. My own lineman tackled me and we lost the game. As I was directed by my lineman to lead the way, he turned back toward me and ran right in to me.

A few weeks later we had the big Thanksgiving Day game against our cross-town rivals Lyman Hall. We were 0 and 9 and nobody was projecting us to win, including us. Some of the seniors were more vocal that week; they wanted to go out on a winning note!

We got the ball first and as I went to hand off to the running back, I was hit and fumbled in our own territory. Lyman Hall took it in for a score. One of the seniors came up and said to me, "If you let that get in your head, we lose!"

I didn't. I ran for a touchdown, which didn't please one of the seniors who said, "You have two more years to score touchdowns, I have one quarter!" I threw for the next touchdown, but we lost the game. I kept thinking it was all about the way we approached the game. Another senior at the end of the game told me, "Don't let this happen next year!" and I understood that life was there for the taking. That one game showed me, if anything, that you play for today, not tomorrow.

Football taught me a lot that year. It raised my social status and opened some doors for me. It also closed others on me. During spring football that year, players and coaches expected more out of me. I was now to be the example, and my actions on and off the field would be viewed by a lot of different eyes. For example, my coaches emphasized grades and behavior in school. I also learned the program was bigger then any individual.

Those forty-eight hours flew by. My road to recovery had begun. Some days it felt like I was walking at a snail's pace; other days it was as though I was racing down the road in a Ferrari. I never even prepared myself for failure; I had too much optimism and faith to think about failing. I had too many people helping me counter my setbacks and showing me new and different approaches when I needed them.

Dr. Frank Palermo was the only doctor who told me what I wanted to hear. He put together a great workout with a recipe for success. He showed me it was not only the major muscles that we needed to strengthen, but the smaller supporting ones as well. Luck and destiny may be the only substitute for hard work. I kept a calendar and would rate the days from one to five. One was a great day with a lot of improvement and five was one with no improvement at all. Although there weren't more then a handful of five days, the days after those days, I would push myself even harder. I came up with the number process to push myself, a five the prior day would make me do five more reps, or hold a stretch for five seconds longer. It's what needed to be done to make up for a lost day. I put myself at no more then a calendar week's worth of fives. If I was to succeed, that needed to be littered with mostly ones and twos. This was a simple, easy system to keep myself on the right track.

As a child, I didn't really like swimming, but the pool became a big part of my recovery. The important thing about the pool was that I could bear full weight on my leg. So I would swim laps and then run laps in the low end. I would do leg kicks to the front, back, and the sides. I would finish with laps again, but this time I would use mostly upper body. The pool had to become my friend in order for me to succeed.

Sometimes we have to do the things that we like the least just to get the edge that we need. A lot of athletes look for anything to give them an advantage, to put them over the top. It is this drive that causes some to turn to performance-enhancing drugs.

Workout machines have their advantages, but there's still something about the blood, sweet, and tears method. I used to put in the training segment of *Rocky II* while I ate breakfast to get myself pumped up for that day's workout. I would be up by 6:30 every morning, eat breakfast, and get to Dr. Palermo's office by eight with my father. They would set me up on an electric stimulation machine. The currents would retrain and strengthen my nerves and the surrounding muscles. They would start with my quads and hamstrings for twenty minutes, then my lower back and gluts. I would isolate every muscle possible, strengthening each one to its maximum performance. Then it was on to a workout with weights. After that, I would return to get electric stimulation on my shoulders and triceps. I would go home, eat lunch, and then I was off to the swimming pool with mom for more therapy.

After the pool rehabilitation a few teachers from my high school tutored me. A lot of people really stepped up to make things easier for me. My school principal bent over backward to work around my rehabilitation. My teachers would always come on time and most times come with milkshakes because they knew I was trying to gain weight. After my tutoring session, I would have dinner, sometimes do a radio interview about my progress, and then wait for my home physical therapist, Tony Rapuano.

Tony always came to work with a positive outlook that made you want to work hard. When Tony left, you felt like not only did you get a physical workout, but a mental one as well. I can't tell you what a boost to the psyche it is to have the people around you be up beat. After working out all day long, it's hard to pick yourself up for another session, but Tony came in and motivated me. At first he would stretch me out. I wasn't a big fan of stretching, so he had his work cut out for him. My left leg was extremely tight because of the month and a half in traction. This had been the most painful and hardest thing to overcome since returning home. I would have never thought stretching a muscle could cause such pain. Tony would make me count to thirty while he would stretch my leg. The pain was so intense I would scream at the top of my lungs. My screams were so loud that my mother would have to leave the house.

I dreaded those stretching sessions so much that I would practice counting to thirty just to lessen the time. Tony was quick to notice the difference and, one night, after having two stretches go by quicker than usual, Tony asked if I could count backward from thirty. Clever trick. It was hard to concentrate with the pain, and that thirty seconds turned into about fifty seconds every time. They say, "No pain, no gain," but this felt like all pain, no gain. I was losing this battle, and doubt started to set in. I was beginning to doubt that I could complete this goal. Again I practiced counting, this time backwards from thirty, trying to do it as fast as possible to spare myself pain. But no matter how fast I counted, the pain was extremely intense. Tony would only do reps of thirty seconds, but one night when he finished I told him to do it again. Three reps in, I felt a pop; the pain was gone and progress was made. Tony said that he was proud of me that night. I faced a fear head on. It probably would have happened in the next week's sessions, but it felt like I had taken a big step forward. It felt like a major accomplishment, as if I had gained ground I didn't think was possible so soon.

With that hurdle behind me, I felt like I had a good pace going and I was ready for what was next. I never told anyone what my progress was in the first five months, especially my friend Matt. The one thing that I didn't want was for us to compete. Our fights were within our own bodies, our own minds. We were in this together, although he couldn't yet remember the night of the accident, we both needed each other to understand that night.

Whenever I talked with Matt, he was always positive, although physically he was very frail. It took him five to six months before he asked me about that night. It was strange to me to explain it to him, he was there, yet couldn't remember anything. Some things I wanted to forget; yet he was searching for answers. It's funny how life works sometimes.

Matt absorbed every detail of that night. As painful as it was, he always made the point that he needed to do it. We all forget times or moments in our lives, but I could see why we would need to fill in those blanks. These were the answers to why his life was altered. Will all the answers to that night reveal themselves; most likely no.

Matt was just happy to be alive. Faith became a major part of our lives and recovery. We both learned a lot about people. Most were unbelievable, wanting to help in any way they could, some would help just to gain information to feed the gossip mill, and some couldn't care a less. At first it was hard to tell who is who and what they wanted. Since Matt couldn't remember anything yet about that night, he was at least spared those questions. That still didn't stop people from prying.

Father Paul, the priest from Marc's church, came into our lives at the right time. Matt and I were searching for answers, so we both jumped at the chance to meet with Father Paul at a local pizza place. We may not have gotten the answers we were looking for, but we did receive friendship. Father Paul then took us to the cemetery where Marc was buried. It was the first time I was there. It seemed so permanent and I discovered that a part of me didn't want to come to the realization that he was gone. It was easier to think he had moved away or gone on vacation. It was tough to see his stone, to accept that he wasn't coming back. I walked away with feelings on both sides of the spectrum. First I was very hurt and couldn't digest the painful feelings. The second feeling was joy, the joy of being alive. I wanted to live life to the fullest, to get the most out of it.

It would have been easy at any point after the accident to start the public relations campaign for my name, but my father said, "Don't get wrapped up in the crap." He was right, but it really didn't matter because two to three months later, no one cared. I had taken my stance, and I wasn't backing up or backing down. It's not always easy to be a better person; sometimes you need to take a stand for your beliefs or values. I wanted my actions to speak for me, to become more than the controversy surrounding me. It's easy to complain. Words are cheap, but results are what speak volumes. Maybe I was too young to get wrapped up in meaningless details, but I had more immediate problems that needed to be addressed. I turned back on my selective hearing that had served me so well in the hospital. I tuned out the hurtful words. Grandmother Lunney used to say, "You can never go wrong by doing the right thing." I was hoping she was right.

The right thing—where did *that* concept go? It certainly didn't exist when it came to the accident investigation. It turned out that there was evidence missing from the accident. People hated me for things I didn't do, and my family members were still trying to catch their breaths from the stomach blow.

So many things changed because of that one night. Not only did they affect me and my family members' lives, but they had an amazing ripple effect on other lives.

Chapter 13

It was now five months after the accident, and also prom time. At first I thought, *who would want to go with me?* But I found out how far from the truth that was when I received calls or letters from twenty or so girls asking me to be their date. At the time, I didn't want to commit to any of them because I didn't know if I would be physically ready to go. The prom is a big investment, and the last thing I wanted to do was ruin someone's night. Would I do it different now? Of course, but hindsight is twenty-twenty. At that time, I still felt I let a lot of people down, I also felt I was only half the person I once was. Adjusting to change is part of life, but as a teenager that's not your mindset.

Working out kept my stress at a minimum and I still had good friends who had my back, but I was a bit stressed out about the prom. It was two weeks before the prom, and I needed to make a choice about whom I was going to take. It turns out; the choice was made for me. Ten minutes before I was going to call the girl I wanted to ask, a friend called me crying because her boyfriend broke up with her and he wasn't taking her to the prom. The next thing I knew, we were going to the prom together. I was happy to have the chance to go with my friend, but I also felt like I was letting the other girls down. I admit I was getting caught up in my image, what people were thinking or saying about me. There were so many girls who had done so much for me that choosing one was impossible. That's why I think God made the choice for me. It was the best-case scenario. This was a blessing in disguise for me, and my friend probably thought *I* was doing *her* a favor.

I can't tell you how often I thought of how lucky I was to survive that accident and to have the opportunities in front of me that I did. My date and I had a lot of fun; we even were crowned the prom king and queen.

The day after the prom we all went to Riverside Amusement Park in Agawam, Massachusetts. I just wanted to take the weekend to unwind. I rode six or seven rides before I saw the sign warning people who had recent surgery to stay off. A bit later, I began to feel pain in my hip. I sat on a bench and told everybody I was just tired and to go have fun. When I got home I just lay on the couch and watched TV.

That Monday, Dr. Palermo had a conference and needed to attend, so I didn't have any therapy or see any doctors until Tony visited at 5:30. Right away Tony noticed my demeanor. After explaining my plight or what I thought was one, I remember him taking my leg and pushing it to the ground. "You're past that point," he exclaimed as he told me my bones were healed and even stronger then before. He then wanted to know if I had any more doubts before we continued. Whether I did or not, I had to put on my best poker face. I had come too far to let my emotions get in the way. My bones were healed, now it was a matter of strengthening my muscles and nerves. I had to place my faith in God; I was here for a reason.

With the prom over, I wanted to limit my distractions, but I also wanted to enjoy life a little. I was a big movie buff so Friday and Saturday nights were movie nights. Sometimes those nights would include a game of mini golf. I would just go with whoever wanted to go. I saw *Batman* seven times in the theater that year. Crazy maybe, but I kept thinking I could escape from reality, could get away from everything that was going on. But I was wrong. It was wild to know how many people were following the story. I would be waiting for tickets and someone would start up a conversation on how things were going and then wish me luck. It never annoyed me no matter how many times it happened. It was just nice to know people cared or were interested in me, whether they wanted to know about the accident or if I would make it back to the field.

July was my make-it-or-break-it month. I continued to work hard on my therapy. Knowing how many people were following the story made me work that much harder. Blood, sweet, and tears had a whole new meaning for me. The pool was incorporated into my workouts because we had a pool at our house and it was convenient. The last place I wanted to be was in that pool, but I made myself use it two or three times a day. The price of recovery has its pains and annoyances.

The one thing I didn't need to work on was throwing. After months of being on walkers, crutches, and a cane, my arms were strong. I didn't even use my plant foot and still was able to throw seventy-five yards. Since the strength was there, I worked on making my release quicker. I had always worked out hard, but had never had quite so much at stake. Each day I worked out harder than the previous day. At this point, time was what became the bigger issue with the football season right around the corner.

As I worked through my therapy, things quieted down a bit. The accident was wrapped up into the legal system; interviews moved to the back burner, probably because at that point nobody knew in which direction I would go. I guess the good thing about doing something next to impossible is that expectations are slim to none. Only God knows what outcome will be.

Chapter 14

As hard as I was working, I was still a seventeen-year-old boy. I wanted a personal life. I wanted a girlfriend. The odd thing was, I couldn't see myself with any of the girls I went to school with. It wasn't that I didn't like them; I just thought that they saw me as something more than I was now, that I would be a disappointment to them. I know now I was wrong, but back then I thought love was perfect. I didn't realize it is actually hard work. I was looking for someone to share my life, someone to pick me up when I faltered. How I was going to find that person, I hadn't a clue. But fate did. Fate knew exactly what was in store for me.

My cousin's girlfriend had a friend she wanted me to meet. With football season right around the corner, and my friend Marc's birthday less then a week away, I decided to roll the dice. Fate had broken my heart, would it be able to fix it, too?

Part Three: Agnes

I met Agnes August 11 1989, on a blind date. The third time is a charm applied to us, nothing to do with her, but I had cold feet. First, her name was tough for me. Second, my cousin's girlfriend said she was pretty, and that could go either way.

Nevertheless, I agreed. We decided on a movie, and my cousin, his girlfriend, and I went to Agnes's apartment to pick her up for our blind date. The moment I saw her, I was done for. She was gorgeous, and I welcomed my heart finally pounding over something other than a workout or a bad situation.

It wasn't her beauty that stood out that night, however; it was her unique personality. I had been raised a gentleman, and I didn't expect my dates to pay their own way. But on this night things were different. When we arrived at the movies, Agnes told me she needed to use the bathroom. Instead, she went in and bought a ticket for me. She reversed the roles and threw me a curveball that I could not get out of my head. It's funny how the little things can mean so much sometimes.

Lock-Up was the first movie we saw together, being on our first date, I thought I should impress her. Attempting to be cool, I was feeding her popcorn; only problem was that a few kernels fell down her tank top. *One date,* I thought, *and I'm done.* But, when it came time for our goodbyes I said I was sorry about the popcorn. She just smiled, kissed my cheek, and said, "We'll talk tomorrow. "Words can't describe the feelings I had. I kept thinking, *Should I even pursue her?* We were from two different worlds. Agnes was born in Poland; I was from small-town USA. Could I make her happy? Well, whether it was fate, destiny, God, or whatever, I chose to follow my heart. It had yet to fail me. Again, see how our minds or people around us almost talk ourselves out of our dreams or the things we want most.

The next day, I brought flowers to her work. Thinking I might ruin my chances if I walked in with my cane, I left it in the car. It wasn't until later that she told me she couldn't get past my smile to even notice my limp. It was only eight months since the accident and for the first time in a long while, I didn't have to paint that smile on my face. I felt blessed to be alive and to have this chance to be with this beautiful woman. Having her at this moment was truly a blessing in more ways then one. She kept me from thinking about all the surrounding stress.

On my birthday two weeks later, Agnes bought me a gold necklace. In the past, my birthday had been all about football. It coincided with either started double sessions or was in the middle of them, so just having her there to celebrate with me was gift enough. She was a welcome addition. I also knew how hard she worked, and the fact that she spent her hard-earned money on me made the gift that much more special. We had known each other for less then a month, but we had a connection that was on a new level for me. We started spending as much time together as we could.

As we were getting to know each other, I sensed that Agnes seemed afraid of getting too close, but at this point I was doing a lot of interviews for the newspapers, radio, and television. She would joke around and say it was hard not to think about me. One of the best things about Agnes was that even though she wasn't a sports fan, she supported me all the way. She understood how important playing was to me and to others. One of the most asked questions by her and others was if I was afraid to get hurt again. Call me young and stupid, but having just recovered from major injuries at an unparalleled pace, I believed I could do it again if I had to. This allowed me to focus on the goal and not the unthinkable in my mind—and being hurt again was unthinkable. Regardless of all the support by the people around me, I had always felt as if the weight of the world was on my shoulders. When I met Agnes, I felt as if the world was at my fingertips.

The next few weeks were taxing on me and on a lot of people around me. Football season began in earnest, and there were some guys who were not happy that I was getting most of the press and I hadn't played a down yet. The locker room began to divide. I couldn't believe it. For three years I don't think anyone worked harder than my friend Chris and I. We believed singer Sammy Hagar when he said, "First the mind - then the soul. And when the heart gets pumped up for goal. There's no defeat . . ." That was us in a nutshell, and still these so-called teammates questioned my heart and my desire. I didn't realize the blessing it truly was because I discovered whom my true friends were. From that point on, there was no looking over my shoulder.

I couldn't understand how they could doubt my heart? Just the year prior when the double sessions (practices from 9:00 a.m. to 8:00 p.m.) began in August, I was in great shape and ready to tackle the leadership role on the team. With only twenty-three players this season, no one could afford to be out of shape or nurse injuries. As teammates, we got to know each other's strengths and weaknesses, which we did our best to overcome or utilize to our advantage. We even competed with the first team we went up against. We marched our first drive right down the field, but only to come up short. Our second drive resulted into a touchdown pass and control of the game. Our defense did its job, and when the offense took the field again, our coach wanted to go for the jugular.

The coach called for a throwback pass to gain a good chunk of yardage. The pressure was on, and I was dropped back. As I turned to throw down the field I noticed my fullback missed his block. I had a pretty quick release so I threw it down the sideline, but at a cost. My thumb got caught in the approaching defender's facemask and broke. I looked down and saw my thumb bent back so far that my thumbnail was touching my wrist. I put my hand between my legs and pulled it through to return it to its normal place. When I got to the sideline, my thumb had swelled up to double its size. The trainer did his best to tape it up, but it was painful to take a snap, and I couldn't throw the ball more than ten yards. I was going to go back out there and just run the ball, but Coach Mannion took my helmet from me. He told me I had more football in me, but not for that night. I wanted to be out there, but I respected his opinion. He knew me, and the game of football. We lost the game, but I learned that I had people behind me who respected me as a person and as a player.

Up to that point in my life, I had never broken a bone in my body. In fact, in class that very afternoon a teacher had asked who had broken any bones. I was the only one who hadn't. This was when I realized to never say never, sometimes you learn the hard way.

For the next two weeks, I was sidelined with my injury, and only entered when someone was hurt on defense. I had a smaller-than-usual cast, but it was still bulky to throw with. After the two-week wait, I was fitted with an even smaller cast. I practiced constantly to adapt to it. During a game, though, I was required to wrap the cast in felt because they didn't want the hard cast to hurt another player. I couldn't get a good grip on the ball this way, so throwing on the run was no longer an option. I took this as just another challenge to overcome, though. It made me a better player because I had to learn to work with less and still succeed. We tend to get complacent with what we have until its no longer there.

Our season wasn't going so great, and we continued to lose every game. Its like we weren't even showing up. The one team we had half a chance of beating, we lost because several of our teammates were caught drinking and were suspended. We went out there with fifteen guys, made a game of it, but came up short in the last drive.

We had two games remaining that season, against two teams that were better than us. For one, we played hard for three quarters before falling short of a victory. The last game of the season was against Lyman Hall, our cross-town rivals, on Thanksgiving Day. It wasn't a point of getting up for this game, but a matter of being prepared. The night before the game we had a terrible practice, we couldn't do anything right. After practice I got yelled at pretty good while my teammates just walked to the locker room. The coach wasn't mad at my performance in practice, but how I ignored the performance of my teammates and just gave them a pass. I understood what he was saying, but I liked to lead by example. In my eyes it was hard to yell at someone who wasn't as dedicated to the sport as I was.

So when school started my senior year, it was a completely different atmosphere for me. All the high school drama didn't mean a thing to me anymore. The little things that used to get under my skin, didn't take up my time anymore. It was tough facing school without Marc, knowing he wouldn't be there to make me laugh. There were days I would walk by his locker and think he was just late to school.

It was almost three years of walking by Marc's locker knowing he would make me laugh. The first few weeks were difficult knowing that he was gone. It took some time, but I finally realized the lifetime of memories he had left me. I kept focusing on what was left behind, as opposed to what was lost.

We all got choked up or even began stories with tears; however, they all ended with a smile. Everyone in the school was effected in some way. Matt and I were not the only ones who needed to heal. I would say this was a compliment to the person Marc was.

Chapter 15

It is my belief that people are put in our paths to get us through certain moments in our lives. Coach Mannion already had my respect as a man and coach, but now he was my teacher. I was fortunate to have a lot of great people who took stock in me and really took me under their wings when it came to education. Coach Mannion had an unconventional way of teaching; he not only taught English, he taught life as well.

Call it fate, but this class was exactly what I needed. Coach was a Vietnam veteran who experienced the ugly side of life. He knew where my friend Matt and I were coming from. He spoke often of his tour in Vietnam where he lost people around him, was injured physically, and had his share of emotional challenges as well. We read *One Flew Over the Cuckoo's Nest*, *Hunchback of Notre Dame*, and *Deliverance,* and Coach Mannion brought each one to life for us and showed us how they pertained to our current life stories.

You had to respect Coach the moment you met him. The books had some questionable material, in the eyes of some and he received some flack for that. He stuck to his guns and taught us that while you can't please everyone, it's important to stand for what you believe in. He definitely kept me on the right path! I can only say I was truly blessed to have such an example right in front of me. He was a model of survival and success on how to endure.

Chapter 16

School was going as well as could be expected, but the first few weeks of football had been frustrating. The season had started and I could do nothing but sit there and watch. I wanted to be out there playing. When I called my Uncle Joe one night after a game, he right away made me focus on a positive. "What were the defenses doing?" he would ask. "What would you have done differently?"

I told him I thought the game looked slow. He said, "Good, you learned something." He told me the sharper I made my mind, the less I would have to expect from my body. I hung up the phone that night and thought about how God had intertwined all these positive people in my life to get me to the next level. Just another example of using what I had and not dwelling on what I had lost.

My uncle, Joe Kuczo, was a trainer for the Washington Redskins and I began what became a close relationship with him during my freshman football season. Between my father and Uncle Joe, I was on a path to perfection. Uncle Joe and Aunt Rosa were two of the most caring and giving people I knew. Just that authentic care for others that is hard to find in people today. My uncle always made time to take my calls. He was a source of positive energy that kept me on my goals. He never let me get down. It seemed as if he took it upon himself to keep my chin up.

I remember my uncle once sent me a huge bottle of vitamin c and an article about Herschel Walker and his workout without weights. The article explained that Walker did 1,000 push-ups and 1,000 sit-ups a day. My uncle thought I should start building up to that. I took his advice and learned to love working out, getting a little better every day. It took me about two weeks to work up to 1,000 sit-ups and about two months to reach the goal of 1,000 push-ups. My uncle always told me that the days you don't want to practice are the ones that will make you great. It took me the better half of a year for the meaning of that statement to sink in, but he was right. My uncle sent me two footballs and some game footage on some of the pro quarterbacks. Respect is one of the greatest accolades we can receive in this life.

Joe Kuczo with Vince Lombardi at Redskin training camp

Sometimes there were supporters where I least expected them. At one game, the coach for Derby High School came over to me at halftime and presented me with a retired Derby football jersey. He told me that he had always appreciated the way I played. That meant a lot to see an opposing team's fans cheer for you. This was the first time I actually thought this was about more than just football. It was often I would think about all the great people who molded me. They provided me with passion, heart and conviction. All the times they helped me, never asking for even a thank you, but only wanting the best from me.

Chapter 17

Three to four times a week Agnes would take walks around the football field with me. We never once talked about football. Our conversations were mostly about the accident and about how I wanted to be a father one day. We were learning to be a part of each other's lives, understanding and adapting to the nuances of a relationship. I give her credit; she was taking stock in something that could have failed. It's funny what others see in us that we sometimes can't.

My therapy was progressing at a decent pace. Surprisingly, for one of my sessions, Doctor Frank Palermo asked me to bring in my football equipment. One of his other patients was a linebacker from Penn State University, and he also helped a handful of hockey players from the New Haven Nighthawks (a semi-pro league).

Dr. Palermo would set up the hockey players at certain pass routes. He would then tell the linebacker to rush after a two count. As I dropped back, Doctor Palermo would yell out a number and I would have to hit that receiver while being driven into the floor by this human missile. I would say I was hit about twenty five times—high, low, in my face, and blindside. The more I was hit, the stronger I felt. The doubt leaving my system was re-energizing my spirit. I was regaining my confidence—in many areas.

Chapter 18

In life there are always a few steps forward countered by a few steps back. I staggered a bit when I heard the news of my Grandfather Lunney's passing. He had been sick from a stroke a few years prior and had lost his ability to speak, and could not move anything on the left side of his body. It had been awful to see a man who never asked for much of anyone require the aid of so many in the last few years of his life. It was a blow to me to lose him no matter how many times people told me it was for the best. Loss is never for the best. I guess you can say it's just better for those who move on.

Agnes was there for me, keeping me on the right track, but as she pushed me toward my return to football, we started to drift apart. About two weeks after my grandfather's funeral, we decided to give each other some space. Although we were no longer a couple, we remained friends. We never went more than three days without talking on the phone and catching up with our lives.

The night before my return to the playing field I was watching an old football tape and trying to relax. The week had been crazy between all the interviews and emotions and I was a ball of stress. Then I got a call from Agnes. The week's chaos came to a halt and I felt my stress unraveling as I listened to her calming voice. I can't imagine how long the night would have been if I hadn't spoken with her.

Soon enough my date with destiny was upon me; it was game time. We were up against Cheshire High School, a powerhouse and a true test of whether I would continue playing or leave the sport I loved.

The game came quick. It was all Cheshire. I watched as the clock ran down to less than five minutes in the forth quarter. When we got the ball back, people in the stands were yelling my name. Goosebumps covered my body as I ran onto the field. As we broke the huddle and I lined up in shotgun formation, I looked to the sky and thanked God for giving me the strength and opportunity to be where I was. I began the cadence. My running back started in motion, but went too far out and wasn't going to be able to block the rushing defender. I didn't think twice, I called for the snap and completed a pass down the sideline. The crowd erupted as we marched down the field with two more completions. My forth ball thrown was intercepted and I could only watch as the cornerback raced down the sideline for a touchdown. I walked to the sideline and all I could think of is that a year ago that defender wouldn't have gotten five yards without me being right there.

We got the ball back with limited time on the clock. I broke the huddle thinking, *This is it.* My buddy George Curry said before he split out, "Let me run short, end on a positive." I knew where he was coming from, but I wanted to go out swinging. I wanted it to be all or nothing. I dropped back, threw down field, watched my last pass fall into the hands of the Cheshire safety. I remember thinking, *So much for the fairytale ending,* but this was life, and as my English teacher Coach Mannion always said, "Life isn't fair!" I had failed, but I didn't *feel* like a failure this time. I had given it everything I had, but I just wasn't the player I had been a year prior.

When the last tick of the clock faded, the crowd was still cheering for me as if I had thrown a winning touchdown. I might have lost the game, but I had won their hearts. The coach from Cheshire shook my hand and told me to keep my chin high, that I had a lot to be proud of. I was too wrapped up in the moment to realize that this could be my last game. I walked off the field wondering where my life was headed.

Agnes was right there waiting for me. As one door closes another one opens. People often refer to life as roller coaster, now I knew exactly what they were talking about. Since January, my life had had its share of peaks and valleys. I believed that while fate may have been responsible for the valleys, I made it up more than a few of those peaks on my own. Even if everyone around you tells you that you can't, as long as you convince yourself that you can, I promise good things will happen. If you give it your all, there will be no doubts, no second-guessing yourself down the road. I know this now, but as an eighteen-year-old high school senior, I still believed that no obstacle was unreachable, that nothing is unattainable.

Chapter 19

Love is the greatest, most powerful thing on this earth. I loved football, but I knew I couldn't play forever. I also knew I wanted to be married young and love forever. That is where pride hurt me; I wanted to give her the world, and at this point of my life I didn't see myself being able to do that. I was confused. I worked my tail off to achieve a goal, and I was beginning to see that dream slip away. My senior yearbook claims I was voted "Most Popular," but throughout that year, there were many times I felt as if I had only a handful of friends and a head full of shattered dreams.

Chapter 20

I didn't allow myself to give up the idea of playing and playing well again. One night I was running in my backyard trying to keep in shape. Even before the accident, I always ran looking at the night sky. This night I was staring at the moon when I noticed it moving up and down. I then realized my gait was changing. I began to notice it more and more.

I tried to disguise my limp by using a cane because I thought maybe I was just over using my leg and it was getting tired. It turns out that was only wishful thinking. As my limp became more pronounced, the doctors determined that the top of my hipbone was losing its blood supply and my own body weight was crushing it. I would need another surgery.

Not only did this mean that my playing days were over; but like I said before my own young, male pride got in my way when it came to Agnes. I wanted to continue our relationship, but I knew that wouldn't be fair to her. I didn't know how long my recovery would be, or what condition I would be in after the next surgery. At the time I thought I had made the right decision, but it wasn't until later that I realized I was wrong.

On Agnes's eighteenth birthday in 1990, I called and left a message for her. When she returned my call the next day, I invited her to dinner. At one point in the dinner she came out and asked, "What are we going to do about your leg?" I told her I needed a year to bounce back, and she answered by saying, "I think we'd be better off doing this together." That was it. We were back together. The fates had deemed it so.

Suddenly we didn't have any single goals, everything was about us. We started working on our future, where we wanted to be, what we would give up to reach our goals. We knew there would be bumps in the road, but it's amazing how your psyche changes about a goal when someone is there with you.

Chapter 21

Soon after I was called to give a deposition for the accident. The girl who caused the crash had already changed her statement at least three times. While it was incredibly hard to relive that night, my friend Matt and I were determined to clear Marc's name. Even though Matt still couldn't recall any of the events of that night, he always kept my spirits high and supported me through this ordeal.

My deposition was a whole new experience for me; I was completely sandbagged. The lawyers started out with these sweet questions, and then dropped the hammer on me. They blamed football for my hip injury. Seriously? The last game I had played in before the accident was on Thanksgiving 1988. The accident and injury occurred in January 1989. They were suggesting that I walked around for two months with a shattered pelvis?

I was questioned by the lawyers from a couple insurance companies as well as lawyers for the girl who caused the accident. For hours they would pry and dig for anything they could use in their favor. Agnes sat next to me the whole time and at moments rubbed my calf with her foot. It meant a lot to me that she was there and, without a doubt, it made things easier again for me. In a way it didn't seem fair that we were just kids and already up against these adult problems. We were up against a trial and a hip surgery when most kids our age were partying, sleeping late, and going to the beach.

Chapter 22

It was about a week after the deposition that I went to see the orthopedic doctor who had performed my two surgeries following the accident. I knew my hip was getting worse, but I didn't know at what rate. At the appointment, I found out that I was walking around with half of my hipbone and would require a hip replacement. The doctor also informed me that he wouldn't perform the surgery because of his age and mine. I was shocked, and told him I would be comfortable with him operating on me. But, he said he would leave the surgery in the hands of someone more capable. Another lesson that life moves on. As I look back now, I understand that he set a high bar for the next doctors. He put my well being before a paycheck. Integrity was the lesson I took home that day.

Over the next two weeks my parents and I met with other doctors who were capable of the surgery. All of them recommended a replacement except one. This one doctor suggested that a hip fusion surgery would also be an option, but there was a drawback. A hip fusion would completely limit mobility and cause me to walk with a limp. I was full of emotions—my family and Agnes were the only constants. I felt cheated. I pondered the fact that life really isn't fair, but at least I was alive. There's a lot of times where I had to convince myself that I was lucky. There were plenty of opportunities out there, it was just a matter of finding them, creating them, or just making the most of them.

My mother never gave up hope One day, she read about this hip specialist in Washington, D.C. who had great results with patients with bad hips. Within a week, we were in the capital area getting other opinion. What was supposed to be an hour-long appointment turned into a six-hour one. Dr. Engh continued to take X-ray after X-ray, reviewing my injury from multiple angles and positions. After he reviewed every x-ray, he came to the same conclusion as the others—I needed a hip fusion. If my parents weren't in the room, I would have cried, but the last thing parents want to see is their child hurt, so I sucked it up. I kept thinking, *Why isn't anything going my way?* I gave him my best sales pitch for the replacement, but he countered with, "If you were my son, I would do the fusion."

The problem was that my hip was now constructed of more metal than bone, so a replacement could be done, but it would be at high risk. A hip replacement at that time could last from ten to twenty years in an older patient. I was approaching my nineteenth birthday, and being far more active than those who would normally receive a hip replacement, I could only bank on mine lasting about ten years. After that, with the state my hip was in, I could get two replacements and possibly three taking into consideration the amount of scar tissue the other surgeries would leave. All of this added up to the possibility of me being in a wheelchair by the time I was forty. I was weighing this against having the hip fusion, which would leave me with a pronounced limp for the rest of my life. At this stage in my life, a hip fusion went against every fiber of my being, but I had to look past *me*, and more to what was down the road for my future family and me.

For the past year and change, my life had been topsy-turvy to say the least. If seem as though not much was going my way, but I had to consider that maybe God had a different plan for me, a bigger picture than I imagined. I guess God was giving me a brand new canvas and I was responsible for what appeared on it. A week after my graduation in 1990, eighteen months after the accident, I scheduled the operation for the hip fusion with the doctor from Washington, D.C. It wasn't what I wanted, but it was necessary.

Agnes and I

Chapter 23

I thought the rigors of surgery and recovery would have brought distance between Agnes and me again, but that wasn't even close to what happened. Deep down, we are all special people with unique gifts, but it's how we use those gifts or if we even choose to use those gifts that define us. Maybe the most important thing Agnes taught me was how to love. I was afraid to put all of my heart into anything again, but she put me in the right place yet again.

The whole week leading up to the surgery, Agnes and I spent just having fun. However, going into this surgery, I was a little more stressed. I had new goals with Agnes on board, and it felt like I had a lot more to lose. The way I saw it, I needed to get past this stage before I could really start a new path. The night before I left for Washington, D.C., for the surgery, Agnes and I were in my backyard discussing our future together. We were young with time and ambitions on our side. Words can't describe the feelings I had for her or the goosebumps I got when she hugged me and told me I would be fine because I was to be her husband.

At the hospital, the night, before the surgery, I called Agnes and we talked from 10:30 p.m. to 4:00 a.m. I can't say if it was nerves or my father's snoring keeping me awake, but either way I knew I needed Agnes's voice to relax me.

The next day, when I was alone in a hallway before the surgery, my mind filled with negative thoughts as my heart raced. I was truly nervous until they gave me a drug that calmed me right down. As far as I knew, the surgery went fine, but there were some rough moments with my hip. The first thing I did when I woke up was call Agnes. This was good for me, but bad for her. I was still drowsy from the sedative, and only said, "Hi, how's it going?" Then I passed out and left her to wonder what happened. She told me she worried for about an hour before she got in touch with my mom. Oops. That was just the beginning of a crazy week, though.

The next day, my cousin came down to keep my spirits up. Normally, anytime my cousin and I got together for an extended period of time, our faces would hurt from laughing so much. Unfortunately the next day, there wasn't much to laugh about. My cousin received a call that his grandfather had passed away and had to leave to attend the funeral. A day later Agnes and my sisters Jen and Jess came down to see if they could cheer me up.

I had developed a huge blood clot in my right leg that the doctors were really worried about. I was beginning to doubt my timing. Little did I know things were about to get worse. The last thing I wanted was to stay in Washington, D.C., any longer than I needed to. The blood clot was delaying my progress and my equilibrium was not allowing me to stand for a prolonged period of time, which would have helped alleviate the clot.

But that wasn't the end of the misery. That Friday my sister Jennifer received a call telling her that her fiancé was killed in a car accident. On Saturday, Agnes got a call saying her mom had a heart attack in New York City. Everybody who had come down to support me; was now back at home in pain themselves. I needed to get back home for them.

That afternoon, I started my uphill battle with renewed vigor. At the time, I thought I was in better shape than I was. Before the doctors would let me go home, I needed to be able to walk a certain distance. I didn't realize the toll the fusion had taken on my body and mind. I thought it would be able to get up and go. I found out how wrong I was when I started down the parallel bars. After about ten steps, I started to lose strength and became dizzy. The next thing I remember was waking up to the smell of an ammonia capsule. Maybe it was the smell, or maybe my will to succeed, but I got up and walked the required distance. I focused on the end of the hall, put aside any pain, and told myself that the wall a hundred feet away was the promise land.

I kept reminding myself that I had been in worse shape before and had held my own then. I knew what it was like to dig deep and accomplish things some would consider impossible. This was a drop in the bucket compared to my last two surgeries.

Chapter 24

I left Washington, D.C. in a full body cast. I was strong enough so the weight didn't affect me, but being that it was summer, it got a little hot in that cast. I used to keep a yardstick around just to scratch the itches inside the cast—and I did my best to stay in the air-conditioned areas.

Throughout the summer, Agnes's commitment to me astonished me. She was there as often as she could be. Most nights she would sleep over, and with her there time went by a lot faster. Enduring the difficult times definitely made our love stronger. One moment I'll never forget was when I lost my balance and fell backwards. Agnes held me up physically as much as mentally; in fact, we held each other up. She was there for me as I was there for her. We started talking about our future, about having children. We needed and wanted each other. From this point on, good or bad, we were in this together.

When you're a kid, you make these crazy plans; everything is so wide open. It doesn't take long for the boundaries to be set, though. It was Agnes's senior year when I bought her an engagement ring. She found out about the ring by mistake when the salesman from the company called and told me the setting was in. Agnes overheard the phone call! It wasn't long before we were at the store looking at her ring. Lucky for me, she could now help pick out the stone; she had much better taste than I did. We left that day with the ring, but it was a while before I gave it to her.

Chapter 25

Things were looking good until I returned to Washington, D.C., to get my cast removed. When they took the x-rays, they noticed the top and bottom had fused just fine, but the middle was the problem. There was a good-sized gap between the top and bottom of my hipbone. They said I needed to give it three more weeks to see if it came together. They made the appointment, and I prepared myself for another surgery. As before, prepare for the worst, but hoped for the best.

When I arrived back home I got more bad news—my father had a golf ball–sized tumor at the stem of his brain. The doctors weren't giving him a very good prognosis. He was advised to get his affairs in order. Things just seemed to go from bad to worse. With the news of my father's health, my problems were put on the back burner for sure.

My friend Father Paul had just returned from a vacation in Madjugorje. He came to our house with a bottle of holy water from his trip. He blessed my father's neck and my hip with it. A week later, my father's x-rays were clear of the tumor. The doctor couldn't explain it any other way other than it being a miracle. I wasn't about to argue with it either! When I went to my next appointment, my hip was completely fused; Father Paul's holy water had worked.

I believe things happen for a reason. Three weeks earlier, things hadn't looked too promising, but I didn't shut down or toss in the towel. I kept my faith in myself and in God. I believe in miracles; I've seen them happen more than once in my life alone. God's grace allowed me some more time with my father. We all took advantage of Dad's new lease on life and spent more time with him. It also got me thinking about being a father myself.

In the odd way that things happen, a month or so later, we found out that Agnes was pregnant. We were young: I was nineteen and she was eighteen. However, after two months, our dreams of parenthood ended, at least for the moment. Agnes had a miscarriage. Some things just aren't meant to be, and you have to accept it and move on. It hurt for a while, but together we got through it. As I had learned already in my short life, things do not always go the way you plan. It took Agnes a few months to see through her grief. I kept driving home to her that it wasn't that we wouldn't be parents; it just wasn't going to be right now. We had a lot of plans for our future, and most of them were far off in the distance.

Chapter 26

It was now September 1991 and the Meriden Police Department finalized their investigation. They claimed that a flat tire, on our car, caused us to cross to the centerline and hit the truck head on. We were all blindsided by their determination. This would change the entire landscape of the trials, both civil and criminal. The District Attorney told us he would have to drop the case due to the new findings. We also learned that some crucial evidence was missing, and my statement alone wouldn't be enough to go to trial. We were reeling from yet another blow.

We couldn't bring Marc back, but clearing his name was something we could do. While those involved didn't agree on everything, we all wanted Marc's name cleared. My mother along with Marc and Matt mothers wrote letters to the state's attorney explaining the circumstances. After looking into the accident for five weeks, the state department reopened the case. Because the state was starting from scratch every detail of the case had to be reexamined, which meant more interviews and depositions for me.

It was impressive the way the state came in and took over the investigation. Things were done quicker and more efficiently. My interview with the investigator was very thorough. I thought the right questions were finally being asked. When I told them about the vodka, that next day they found it in a bush down the next street. Although much time had passed, the truth hadn't changed. Suddenly it felt as if someone had my back and we could finally wrap this trial up. The accused girl continued on her course regardless of the state's involvement. Things were getting better, but it was still our burden to prove our side of the story. The scales started to tip in our favor when the girl changed her story yet again. When your chances are slim to none, you hold on to the slightest glimmer of hope. Our case certainly wasn't a slam-dunk, but someone was now pushing us in the right direction.

I wasn't looking to the trial for closure; I had already rearranged things in my life to allow me to move on. Clearing Marc's name and seeing the trial through was something I wanted to do, not something I had to do. The only thing we were going to achieve was justice. Everything else wasn't going to magically disappear because of a positive outcome. This was all new ground for me, so I prepared myself for either outcome. In my heart, I knew the truth, and no judge or jury could tell me otherwise. All I wanted was to walk away saying that I had done everything in my power to clear my friend Marc's name.

Part Three: The Trial

Chapter 26

The days leading up to the trial were stressful. Marc's name was on the line; he was being accused of something he didn't do. Four weeks before the trial, Matt had regained his memory of that night. He was now a man on a mission finally to set the record straight. Between the District Attorney and our own lawyers, the days prior to the trial were packed with meetings. We were hammered with questions and briefed on procedures we would encounter during the trial. As painful as it was, we were going to have to relive a lot of painful memories to accomplish what we needed to do. I started taking long drives at night to clear my head. I put myself in that witness stand in my head constantly. I didn't want my story twisted, and I didn't want to fumble my words because I wasn't prepared.

Agnes was right there by my side, supporting me in every way possible. She would read through previous transcripts and ask me the questions the opposing lawyers had thrown at me. She would phrase the questions differently every time to keep me on my toes. One of the questions was whether I had ever ridden in a car with a flat tire. At the time of my deposition I had answered, "No." Agnes quickly pointed out that I had once told her a story about when my cousin and I were in his car when his front tire blew out. This would throw a wrench into the defense's theory that a flat tire was to blame. I could now say a blown tire wasn't the reason we crossed over the line that night. That is, as long as my testimony was believable.

By the time of the trial, I was as prepared as I would ever be. Unaware of how a trial goes, I thought I would be testifying on Day 1. How was I to know that it would take two days to pick a jury? Then another half day to go over the stipulations, one of which included not mentioning alcohol in the same breath as one of the kid's names. I thought just the opposite, that it would be good to do this. I believed that a story in the newspapers might get kids to realize the devastation of drinking and driving. Like I said, I was confused. Marc and a man from the truck were dead, and countless lives had been affected, yet the cause of the accident couldn't be mentioned.

The legal system seemed to favor the accused, the girl lied, changed her statement, and didn't have an ounce of remorse, yet it seemed as if she had the system wrapped around her finger. Don't get me wrong; she wasn't a terrible person. She was a kid who messed up and didn't want to own up to it. Did I want her to serve a jail sentence? No. I put myself in her shoes; she had made a mistake, a big one. Do I blame her for changing her statement and lying? Not really, she was frightened and so young. Besides who knows what the people around her were telling her. It is easy to jump to conclusions, or assume what is going on in someone's life or mind. My compassion stopped there, though. We were here because she wouldn't own up to her mistake and Marc wasn't going to take the fall for this.

I knew I'd never forget the accident, but I was eager to turn the page and start a new chapter. I imagine anybody involved in a similar situation would want the same thing, so if there is ever an option not to prolong the course of justice, then the legal system should jump all over it. The longer it is prolonged, the larger the sentence or settlement should be. This would certainly speed up the process and spare a lot of people the heartache of living in the past and not being able to live for today.

Tension was high that first week and all throughout the trial. I couldn't imagine what Matt was going through. Matt's heart was working at thirty five percent and every beat had to concern him. Yes, his bones and wounds were healed and of no concern, but his heart and newfound memory was what worried me. It was a waiting game for us; we weren't allowed to join the proceedings until we testified.

We were in a room with two Meriden cops. When the younger of the two was called to testify, the older officer began to question us. It felt first like we were being interrogated, but he wasn't against us; he just wanted the truth. I told him his department lost evidence. I also told him about the connection to the accused girl's grandfather. At first he didn't want to believe it, but he said he would look into it.

The court took a recess for a lunch break. When we returned, it was the older cop's turn to testify. Right before we left the room, the older officer told us that he had looked into things and that we were right. Matt and I were the only other two in the room.

As we were getting ready to enter the courtroom, Matt told me he was happy that this day was finally here. The conversation then quickly moved to football and he told me how he wanted to play one more game. I told him in his condition it wouldn't be worth it. Then I thought to myself, *who am I to be telling him this?* He went on to tell me he was sick of taking eighteen pills every day and still not being close to a 100 percent. At the time, I thought he was just venting, trying to relieve some of the stress, so I wasn't looking too deeply into what he was saying. When he left the room to testify, I thought back on all the good times we had had playing sports, in the classrooms, and just hanging out. My advice is to enjoy every second while you can.

His testimony was long and the day ended with him finishing with what he had set out to do. He looked relieved and his smile said it all. We shook hands and said goodbye.

Later that night, I received a call from my mother. Matt was in a coma. When I arrived at the hospital, Matt was being kept alive by machines. Agnes and I went into his room and prayed. After a few minutes, she left to give me a couple minutes alone with him. Matt was motionless. As I was thanking him for all the good times we had, his arm raised up. I ran out and told the doctor, in hopes they had misdiagnosed the situation. He told me that the movement was just caused by nerves, but I knew better. In my heart I knew it was my friend's way of saying goodbye. Matt decided to play a game of flag football that night.

Before we left, one of Matt's college buddies came up to me and said, "You should have seen him play, he was awesome!" Apparently, Matt had himself a game. This college buddy went on to tell me that Matt had said he had a lot of fun. Then as he began to walk off the field he collapsed and couldn't be revived. I thought about what Matt had told me hours before, in the courthouse. Why had I not made the connection? I was upset that I didn't see the writing on the wall. I wondered if he had wanted me to talk him out of it, or maybe the memories of that night were too much for him. All I do know is that he left this life happy, without any fear of the next life. There were too many questions that I couldn't find the answers to that night. Life was almost too much. Agnes held me and rubbed my head until I went to sleep.

I woke up the next day and put things into perspective. This was my day to testify, but we were given a few days to mourn. Matt's death completely blindsided me. I knew his time might have been limited, but not that soon. His wake was hard on me. He was the only one that would understand what happened the way I did. When I knelt down to pray, I noticed a purple heart in the coffin with Matt. Our football coach/English teacher, Dennis Mannion gave it to Matt. It meant a lot to me because I knew Matt had always wanted to be in the Navy.

The last thing in the world that I wanted to do was face Matt's parents. With that lump in my throat and the tears welling up in my eyes, I stood up and made my way toward them. I felt guilty, not for anything I did, just because we were in the same car and I was now the only survivor. Before I could even say anything, Matt's mother said to me, "Don't cry, you were the tough one." Looking back now, it took a lot of character for her to think about me at that moment. The last thing I wanted to do was let her down, so I said my condolences and left. I would have stayed, but I didn't want to become a painful image of what they lost.

Some people probably thought that I was cold and insensitive, but they didn't understand. Although I wasn't on a football field anymore, most people put me high on a pedestal. People still appreciated my drive to succeed; they didn't want to see me fall or fail. Regardless of what people thought, I felt I needed to live everyday to the fullest in order to honor my two friends. Matt died doing something that he loved. How many people can say that?

The next day at Matt's funeral, I was reminded how fragile life is. Being at his funeral changed things for me. I left the cemetery that day, and set new goals for myself. The first of which was to finish the trial. I felt now I needed to do this for both my friends. With all that Matt was dealt with, he continued to smile and make the most of things. I can only thank him for being that example for me and many others.

Chapter 27

When the trial continued, the atmosphere was different. With Matt's death, there was talk about charging the girl with another count of vehicular manslaughter. The judge didn't include a new charge and the coarse was set, full steam ahead. The exception being this time I didn't have the status of victim; I had become the aggressor. I was sworn in, and the questions started on the easier side. I was incredulous, though, when, as I was describing the events of that night, the girl laughed when I described the way I saw my friend after the accident. My compassion turned into disgust. I had to calm myself down; I couldn't let my anger cloud my thoughts. I was there to clear Marc's name and I wasn't going to let her get into my head.

Lawyers can be sneaky sons of bitches; the girl's lawyer was no exception. She kept trying to bait me into saying something about the bottle of vodka that I saw in the girl's pocketbook, but I remembered the judge's orders that there would be no mention of alcohol surrounding the high school kids.

"What was in her pocketbook?" her lawyer asked. She knew I couldn't answer with the truth, but that didn't stop her from trying. She then asked, "Could it have been a kitty cat?" I answered the only way that I saw fit, I said "No, but it might make you purr."

The judge stopped us right there and had her change her questions. She right away attacked my character, asking about the condoms on the floor in my car. My brother-in-law had bought me a box that I kept in my jacket pocket. They must have fallen out during the impact of the collision. The courtroom went silent, and all eyes were on me.

Regardless of why the condoms were there, it looked bad. It gave the impression that we hadn't been on our way home that night, and that maybe there were holes in our statements. A week earlier I might have cracked under the pressure, but now things were in a whole new perspective. We were the victims, but I would be damned if I was about to get victimized on the stand. There was nothing this lawyer could say that would lead me down the wrong path. My story had been constant from day one. The only way they could win was to shoot me down, and that wasn't happening.

The lawyer's attacks on me became personal in my eyes. She didn't know my friends, and she certainly didn't know what we had gone through and what we still had to face. As far as the condoms went, I just told the truth. I didn't find the girl attractive and I wasn't a drinker, so that hadn't impressed me that night. I answered quickly and made eye contact with the lawyer so people knew I wasn't hiding behind any lies. It didn't matter how this lawyer phrased her questions, she couldn't throw me. Agnes had prepared me well. Even when she tried to jam the tire issue down my throat, I fielded her questions. All day long I felt as if I was swimming with the tide. She hit me with everything she had, and I never missed a beat.

My questioning wrapped up and I left the stand. Apparently, however, the defendant's boyfriend took exception to what was said about her. His intention was to get my attention. The next thing I knew, my sister pushed the girl's father and we were quickly escorted down to the D.A.'s office. I expected to get reamed out, but the D.A. didn't say anything about what just occurred; he was more impressed with how I did on the stand. He said I did great. Things were looking good for us.

After two days of witnesses from the state, both sides completed their closing arguments. The jury didn't take much time at all to deliberate and they came back with the guilty verdict that we wanted. The lost evidence and the lies they told were all seen for what they were. The sentencing was a stomach punch though—the girl received six months suspended license and 1,000 hours of community service. That seemed like a small price to pay for three young lives.

On top of that, about two months after the verdict, the girl was caught violating her probation by driving. She also completed the 1,000 hours of community service in one week. I don't know who signed off on that paper? Regardless of which, She may have been mocking man's laws, but I believe there's a higher power she will face one day. I can be secure in the knowledge that we did get what we were truly there for—we cleared Marc's name. When I walked out of that courthouse that day, I felt like I had a new lease on life. It was a new beginning and it was brighter than I had envisioned it three years prior. I couldn't even think of complaining; my two friends under twenty years old were now dead and only God's grace had kept me alive. I don't know why it happened to us. I also don't know if I'll ever learn the reason I'm still here. Does it matter? I guess some people would want the answer, but the answer isn't going to change the outcome. I lost physically, but won mentally. It was time to start fresh.

Thanks to social media, Kristin Muir and I have become friends. Kristin was a passenger in the other vehicle that night. I always wanted to talk to her again. We do talk about that night, but it's not the focus of our conversations. Although January 20 will always link our lives, I hope the lives we have built after that night are what we are remembered for. She is now a Meriden police officer and a loving mother to her son. There will never be a happy ending to that night, but it's good to know there were happy outcomes.

Chapter 28

With the experience of the trial behind me, I wanted a family more than ever now. I desperately wanted to marry Agnes; it was time to start this new phase of my life.

I returned from an appointment with Doctor Engh in Washington, D.C. I called Agnes from the airport and told her I was starving and wanted to go out to eat. She asked how the appointment went, so I told a little white lie and said we'd talk about it at dinner, just to ensure that she'd come. I know it wasn't nice to play with her emotions, but I wanted that night to be special, and I didn't want to give her any indication of what was coming.

She got all dressed up to take my mind off what she thought was the next hurdle. I picked her up and took her to a restaurant called Septembers. After we placed our order, Agnes asked what I had found out at the doctors. I was holding her hand under the table and said, "I don't know where tomorrow is going to take us, but I know I want you to be right there with me." Then I asked her to marry me. She said yes and then completely surprised me. She wasn't a big fan of public displays, but she leaned over and kissed me. That new door was wide open for both of us; ready, go.

A week later we had joint bank accounts and credit cards. The trial was over, but the civil part of the accident was still going on. I wanted it to wrap up, so I could get the money and buy a house. The whole legal system was new to me, but it didn't seem fair that we had to wait. I just wanted it done, so I could put the past behind me and start over with what I had.

But the process could not be sped up. It is what it is, so we went with what we had. Was I going to be able to provide the way I wanted to? No, but just like in basketball, I compensated in other ways. If I couldn't shoot, I would be the fastest man on the team. I would still be a valuable team player.

Traveling was something we had always wanted to do, and Florida become out choice of vacation spots. Florida had everything we needed—Disney, Universal

Studios, and beaches. Agnes loved to lie in the sun and get a tan. We decided to have a little fun, enjoy life. It was time to make some good memories to replace the nightmares.

Chapter 29

Back at home: Coach Mannion had taken over the head coach position at Sheehan. He said I had an open door if I ever decided to take a position on the staff. At that time I declined his offer. I loved football and would have loved coaching with him, but the timing wasn't right. There were still guys I played with on the team and that weighed a lot in my decision. I also didn't want to ignite any remaining embers about playing. In my eyes, the only positive aspect would have been being able to work with Coach Mannion. But, I couldn't give the game my heart, and the last thing I wanted to do was let coach Mannion down.

Football gave me a lot, but it couldn't compare to the life, love, and the gifts Agnes would give me. It was a new horizon for us, something a little bigger than a game. God had a new plan for Agnes and me. We spent a lot of time together and never listened to people who told us we needed to have our own time. We never felt smothered by each other.

That summer, my father bought us a hot dog cart. That was our job for the summer. On our first day, we made $160. Then, that was it. We never made more than $50 a day the rest of the summer; it didn't matter to us because we were together.

We also took advice from one of our older customers. He told us never to go to bed mad at each other. As odd as it seems, I can truly say we never did. There were two things we agreed we'd never do, one was to go to bed mad, and the other was never to hang up the phone on each other. She understood that I had experienced how fragile life was, and I didn't ever want our last conversation to end on a bad note.

Agnes was beautiful and had modeled for a year before we met. In 1988, another opportunity arose for her to do it again. She had been chosen from a model search. She went to one shoot, and spent the better part of a day there. When it was over, she said she had more reservations than desire. She felt more family-oriented now, and just really had her mind on starting a family. It seemed like the things we could create together greatly outweighed the things we could do as individuals.

We were as ready as we were going to be as far as being parents. When Agnes thought she might be pregnant, I talked my cousin into buying the pregnancy tests for me. He was standing in line waiting when he noticed his girlfriend's mother was right behind him. Talk about your awkward moment!

Even though the test came up positive, Agnes didn't want to jump to any conclusions. She wanted to wait three months before saying anything to anyone. We had no problem keeping our secret in Connecticut. The layers of clothing easily hid any baby bump that might have been showing. However, when we took our annual trip to Florida, our secret was out. We were going to the beach with my friend Casey Dillon when we stopped off at a convenience store.

"Is there something you're not telling me?" Casey asked me.

I explained Agnes' weight gain by saying, "She's been drinking a lot of beer and now she has a beer belly." He told me I might want to think of another story to tell the parents.

Women understand that three-month window better than men do. The fact that the baby survived the first three months was a blessing. To me, it was like winning the lottery. Was I nervous to tell my parents? Yes, mainly because we weren't married yet. But the way I looked at it, two hearts make a marriage, not a piece of paper or two wedding bands. Agnes and I were family-oriented and this is what I wanted from the moment they extracted me from that car. We sat down and told our parents, and when it was all said and done, things went better then we expected.

The first eight months went by so fast, but the last month dragged on forever! Agnes was a trooper, she never complained during her pregnancy. When she started to go into labor, we drove to New Britain Hospital. We were there for about three hours before they sent us back home. After about an hour at home we went back to the hospital. We still had a while before the baby's arrival, but being her first time experiencing labor, I know Agnes didn't want to take any chances. They admitted her, and we walked up and down the hallways to try to get her labor progressing, but this baby just wasn't ready to come out.

We settled into the hospital room for a while. Finally, it was go time and they were bringing Agnes into the delivery room. They wheeled her out so fast that they left me in the dust. I had been lying on the floor next to the air conditioning unit. All I can tell you is that cold air and a fused hip are not a good combination. I was so stiff, that it took me at least two minutes to get to my feet. All I heard was Agnes saying that she was only having one child before she left the room.

I didn't know where they brought her, and I wasn't getting there in any hurry. I was leaning against the wall in the hallway when a nurse came to find me. I told her the situation I was in and she went to get me a blanket. I walked into the delivery room with this huge blanket wrapped around me and Agnes laughed at me! At least me looking like an idiot took her mind off the pain for a minute.

A little after eight in the morning, we were about to experience the miracle of birth. After twenty-four hours of labor, our little Billy decided to make his entrance—and my life changed forever. It was the greatest feeling in the world. There was no going back; we were responsible for another life.

Once Billy and Agnes were settled, I went home to get a change of clothes and eat breakfast. On the way home I listened to Harry Chapin's "The Cats in the Cradle." That song had so much meaning to me. I kept thinking this is why I survived the car accident; this little boy has brought a new purpose to my life.

With Agnes recovering from the birth, I went out to get a job. I found out appearance does matter. I wasn't as religious with my therapy as I should have been and it showed. My limp grew more profound and that unfortunately hurt my chances of getting a job.

I did land a job at a local video store and met one of my best friends. Cindy, who was the manager at the time, saw something in me that others refused to see. She's one of the nicest people I know with a heart of gold. Once again a person who would make a positive impact on my life was placed right in front of me.

Most days when I went home to our apartment in Meriden, Agnes would bring Billy out to the car for me. He loved driving around in circles in the car with me. I can't tell you how good that felt to see them waiting there for me. Those moments are priceless and, hopefully, he will someday share a moment like that with his own child.

Life was different for us now that we had Billy. We never went out, but now we focused on our child, our family. Everything took the backseat to parenthood, including my therapy. The hours a day I used to spend working out turned into hours a week, then only hours a month. I was focused on what I had, not what I didn't have anymore.

Chapter 30

Agnes and I started planning our wedding. The way we saw it, since we had been living together for two years, we had adjusted to each other's imperfections. We definitely had an unconventional approach to marriage, some said we did it backwards, but we knew we had what really mattered—love and communication. We raised a few eyebrows, but we knew what we had, so ignored anyone who passed judgment on us.

As any guy needs to learn, I learned that the wedding day is definitely the woman's day. When we went to pick out our invitations, we both liked the first one. Thinking, *That was easy,* I got up and was ready to leave.

"Where are you going?" Agnes asked.

"That's a good one, we both like it," I said.

But, no, she then convinced me to go through numerous books to see what else there was. An hour and a half later, we had picked out our invitation—the first one we'd seen.

Truth be told, regardless of whether I liked any of the other choices, there was no going back. I had to make my stand. I even pointed out every imperfection all those other cards had. I think the only thing people care about is the food anyway.

We both wanted simple wedding bands; we were in and out of the jewelers in a half hour. After that, my services were pretty much over with the exception of picking out my tux.

I did fine with the tux, except that I forgot to tell the shop owner that my left leg was a half-inch shorter than my right. After the forth time measuring my legs he stood up shaking his head. "I've been doing this for thirty-four years," he said. "Your left leg keeps coming up an inch shorter." He was somewhere between mad and relieved after I told him.

About two weeks before the wedding, I had a deposition with the insurance companies. They questioned me for about ten minutes, and then told my lawyer and me that they would work out a settlement. I was happy because we would have more money for our honeymoon. The next day I signed the settlement papers and thought I would have a check by the end of the week. I didn't. It wasn't until four hours before I got married that my lawyer wrote out two checks, one to the bank and one for the honeymoon.

Agnes didn't know about the settlement until after we returned from the honeymoon. I hadn't wanted to add any stress before or on her wedding day.

The wedding itself was perfect. We were married on Friday, October 14, 1994, by our friend Father Paul. Every weatherman predicted rain that day, but after a few brief showers in the morning, the sun broke through and it was beautiful.

Our son Billy, right around fifteen months, wearing a little tuxedo, slept through the ceremony and was wired for the rest of the night. During our first dance together, Billy ran to us on the dance floor. I picked him up and the three of us finished the dance as a family. We took Billy with us on our honeymoon to Florida. We both agreed it would be too many days to be without him. I have never regretted that decision.

While on our honeymoon, we saw and fell in love with a china set. It didn't matter to us that we didn't even have a house. We purchased the set and had most of it shipped home, with the exception of two bags. For our flight home, we needed to switch planes in Atlanta Airport. We had all our luggage, Billy, and two bags of china—and an hour to get from one plane to the other. At first we thought we had plenty of time, but that airport is huge! We were almost to our terminal when Agnes had a hard time getting on the escalator with the two bags. I was at the bottom and was going to leave my two suitcases to go back up and help her when this cowboy took the two bags and carried them down the escalator for her. He placed them next to me, tipped his hat, and said, "Have a nice day." People forget what a random act of kindness can mean. So many people walked by that day and did nothing. This guy, without a second's hesitation, helped us out. That was something that always stayed with us.

We returned home with the bond between us stronger than ever. We had always wanted to have more children and not long after we returned home, Agnes was pregnant again. She carried for about two months before miscarrying. Some things aren't meant to be. The miscarriage threw us for a little bit, but we tried again and on April 23, 1996, our son Jeremy was born. Jeremy was an easy pregnancy for Agnes, but a little rough on me. When Agnes went into labor with Jeremy, I had been working in the yard cutting down oak trees. I had asked Agnes if she thought she would deliver that week and she assured me she wouldn't, so I went to work on the yard not noticing the abundant poison ivy. My entire upper body was soon covered in poison ivy. I remember lying on the couch hoping I would be able to sleep and not be up all night itching like the last two nights. About ten minutes later, Agnes came down and said, "It's time." I guess the choice wasn't hers to make.

Twenty minutes later we were in the hospital waiting for our little boy. Everything went pretty smoothly except for a fifteen-minute span of time where Agnes' blood pressure was elevating. The two nurses were rushing around the room frantically when the doctor came in and adjusted one of the tubes. Everything returned to normal. A few hours later Jeremy entered the world. It amazed me, as it had with Billy, how perfect he looked. It also made me think of the good that came out of the accident, how it all must have happened for a reason. There were so many people who told me God had a plan for me. I knew now that they were right. My children and Agnes brought so much to my life. They took my mind off of my personal struggles and pain.

Chapter 31

Just like anything, there are always expectations, but from the day our children were born, Agnes and I wanted better for them.

Even at a young age, Jeremy was an easygoing child, full of life and love. I used to think, *Wow, two boys!* I had always wanted a brother. It was strange to see two children, from the same two people, be so completely different, but that keeps things interesting. It's like they say, they both follow the same star, but take different directions to get there. I hope they use their gifts to the fullest and allow their shortcomings to keep them humble.

Things were quiet for us; everyday seemed like a mirror image of the next. We had the childcare routine down to a science. It was just a normal quiet life. Even though we had a pretty decent gym in my house, I didn't utilize it as much as I should. Even my doctor's visits became fewer and farther between. I certainly didn't care about what people thought or if they judged me because of the way I walked. Surgery was the alternative, but not an option at this point. My two gifts from God were all I needed to keep myself from dwelling on the pain. I still took the good days with the bad, and always think it could be worse. There were many times when I was told that I was a great example for my children, but the truth was, they set the bar for me. My children brought out the best in me; I became a much better person, I grew with them and will continue to grow with them as life goes on.

I understood my boys; then I had a daughter. It was June 25,1998, when Casey joined our family. Girls are different. You learn that quickly. All of a sudden, pink became very popular and visible around the house. For whatever reason, my approach to parenting for a girl is totally different than with the boys. Did I go easier on my daughter than I did on my boys? Yes, but they'll understand when they have girls of their own someday.

Casey, Billy and Jeremy at Cape Cod

Part 4: Danielle

Chapter 32

Dreams have always played a big part in my life. When I was younger, I had a dream that my Grandfather Gannon was going to pass away on Christmas day (he died on December 26). I had also had a premonition that I would be in a car accident; it was nothing concrete, just a feeling. On April 9, 2001, both Agnes and I had a dream that our daughter Dani would die.

Agnes was nine months pregnant with Danielle. Other then the fact that Agnes was a little heavier all was normal. Agnes went through a battery of tests, but all seemed okay. We were laying two feet from each other experiencing the unthinkable for any parent, yet we kept it from each other. If I had to go through the same thing again, I still wouldn't say anything. I don't remember closing my eyes after 2:00 a.m. It was one of those nights when no matter what position you try, no matter how many times you flip your pillow you just can't get to sleep. When 5:30 a.m. came around, I couldn't have been happier. We got up, showered, and were on our way to the hospital.

We checked in and we were in our room by 6:30 a.m. They started Agnes on Pitocin to induce the pregnancy. The nurses during the day were very nice and extremely helpful. The female doctor broke Agnes's water and raised the Pitocin level. It wasn't long before Agnes was nine and a half inches dilated. With the other births, by the time she reached this point, she was only a half hour away from delivery. We thought within the hour we would have had our fourth child. But then Agnes developed a temperature. The doctor got the temperature to stabilize but she didn't want to deliver or make any decisions because the other doctor was going to replace her shortly.

At 5:30 p.m., a male doctor came in and stated, "You had the rest, now you've got the best." He told us she could deliver the baby naturally. By 7:00 p.m. I called my sister Maureen, the nurse. I related the events so far and she was concerned about the amount of time Agnes had been on Pitocin. She thought we should ask to have a C-section. We asked the doctor when he came in the room at 7:30 p.m.; he denied our request and reiterated that Agnes could deliver naturally and that she should stop "wimping out."

Things then went from bad to worse. Between 7:30 and 9:00 p.m. the staff was hardly there. Agnes needed a catheter because she could no longer get up. After waiting ten minutes for the nurse, I found her in the hallway talking about personal things; she hadn't even gotten the kit yet. After she catheterized Agnes, she had to bring the urine sample to the lab to see if an infection had developed. Again, the nurse was gone for so long that I had to change the bed pads for Agnes two times. This was unacceptable. I didn't mind doing the work, but I felt Agnes was not getting the care she needed.

It was after 9:00 p.m. when the doctor finally came back into the room. Labor had progressed and I could actually see Dani's head. Agnes was told to start pushing. After four or five pushes, the doctor turned to leave. When I asked him where he was going, he said, "I get too hyped up and excited, keep pushing."

The nurse came in for about five minutes and then she left. Agnes was left to push by herself with only me to watch over what was happening.

During her labor, I really saw how strong a woman she was. Agnes was giving everything she had. She was trying so hard that she began to vomit. With nobody around, I held the tray for her. I could tell by the look on her face that she was scared. By 10:00 p.m., she began to feel horrendous pain under her left breast. We found out later that this was an indication that her uterus was thinning out due to the amount of Pitocin she had been given. The doctor should have been concerned about this pain, but he was apparently preoccupied with the vacation he was leaving for in two days, so we found out later.

Eventually, the Doctor ordered another dose of the epidural and two shots of Fentanyl to relieve Agnes's pain. She continued to push, but got only temporary relief from the drugs. The doctor was beside himself, thinking she was giving up. I told him that this was our fourth child and she did fine every other time. Something was wrong!

The anesthesiologist who was there administering the epidural told me that Agnes wouldn't feel anything if they performed a C-section due to the amount of drugs she had been given. I found out later that you will still feel pain in this situation because your body is telling you that something's wrong.

It was a little after 11:00 p.m. when the doctor finally gave the okay to do the C-section. They removed the external monitor, but never set up the internal monitor. This kept everyone in the dark when it came to Danielle's vital signs. The clock struck midnight and it was now April 11, 2001, and by far the worst day of my life. I remember being happy for about fifteen minutes. They were preparing Agnes for the C-section in another room. I was getting changed into hospital scrubs, thinking how neat it was going to be that my daughter Danielle Mary was going to share my sister Maryanne's birthday.

That joy was cut short when nurses urged me to get into the delivery room. Moments after entering, the doctors started the procedure. I was rubbing Agnes' hair with my left hand as we held each other's right hands. My wife once again showed me how strong a woman she was when she kissed my hand. This coming from a woman who was considered a wimp by the doctor making the incision.

Moments later the unspeakable happened. When the doctor lifted Danielle from Agnes, I immediately got an empty feeling in my chest. My daughter's coloring confirmed my fear. She was blue and motionless. With the exception of the delivering doctor, the rest of the medical staff rushed our little girl to the newborn station. I realized how fragile her condition was when they immediately began C.P.R. and began to pump saline into her veins. I blocked my wife's view of our daughter to spare her from having that image. It seems like we always remember the best of times and the worst of times in vivid detail, and only and bits and pieces of what's in between.

Suddenly, a voice over the intercom asked, "What was the time of birth?"

One of the attending answered, "Give us a few minutes."

Agnes finally knew the situation wasn't in our favor. She kept crying out, "I want my baby." As bad as it was for me, I can't imagine how it must have felt for her. For a mother to carry a child for nine months, to feel it moving inside her, and then know that she is losing her; I can't imagine those emotions, that pain. Hope faded with every passing moment.

Twenty minutes passed. A hospital director came in, assessed the situation, and instructed us to make the decision to either keep resuscitating Dani or to make the worst call a parent can make. Despite the best efforts of the hospital staff, twenty-one minutes had passed. If there is no blood flow to a human brain for twenty minutes, the chances of brain damage are high. The director informed us that our best option was to cease resuscitation. Instantly Agnes tightened her grip on my hand, I remember looking into her eyes as she asked, "What do we do?"

"Do we have a choice?" I said, tears welling in my eyes. "We have to let her go." The worst words I've ever had to say.

The director asked again if we wanted them to stop resuscitating. We told them to stop.

As low as I felt, my concern immediately turned to Agnes whom I was told had lost a lot of blood and was two minutes away from bleeding to death herself. I was escorted from the room as they worked to stabilize her. As I was leaving, I crossed paths with the doctor who was responsible for all this. Imagine the only hope of my wife's survival was now in the hands of the man who just killed my daughter. He started to tell me that Agnes was in very poor condition, that she needed surgery, and that she might not pull through. The coldness of his tone shocked me.

"I have to go tell my kids they've lost a sister," I said. "I'm not about to tell them they've also lost a mother." I looked back at my wife as she continued to scream for her baby daughter. I wondered if this would be the last time I would see her alive. Before I left the room I asked God to give this cold doctor whatever he needed to save Agnes's life.

As I proceeded down the hall, one of the nurses hugged me. She walked me to our room and asked if I needed anything. I asked her if she could get a priest for me. Being one of the nicer nurses, she was on her way immediately. I wanted to wake up from this nightmare, but I knew all too well that I wasn't dreaming. After about five minutes, they brought Danielle into the room.

Days earlier I had watched a TV show on miracles. I remembered a child being revived in his father's arms by focusing his energy into the child's body. For fifteen minutes, I tried to channel all my energy into Dani. I wanted to trade places with her, but God had a different plan for us both. For the next fifteen minutes I held her in my arms picturing the life she wouldn't have. From Baptism to birthdays, communion to confirmation, and to the father and daughter dance we would never share.

The Priest arrived and blessed and baptized my little girl. After he said a few prayers for her, the nurse came in to take her for a procedure. The priest looked tired, so I told him to go. Everything was quiet. I remember holding the blanket they would have wrapped her in. My mind was all over the place. I thought about Agnes, I wondered how I would tell my kids they lost a sister, and of course I thought about Danielle. At this point I had gotten no word on how Agnes was.

The first call I made was to my parents' house. My mother was caring for our elderly neighbors and was not home, but my father, who had a dilated pupil and could hardly see, somehow managed to locate the number for me. I know after I told him, he would have walked over to get her for me.

After breaking the sad news to my mother, I had to address the issue of telling my mother-in-law. Agnes's mother only spoke broken English, and I only spoke broken Polish. When you have a conversation this way, you tend to focus on the words you understand the best. I felt she would be stuck on the word *dead* and I wouldn't be able to calm her down. She had a bad heart and was a very nervous person. I felt the only thing I could do is call my sister-in-law, Brenda, and have her explain the situation to my mother-in-law. Again, at this point I was still unaware of Agnes' condition.

Everything was blowing up around me. The nurse returned to my room, she then brought me to a room outside of the maternity ward. She put Dani into my arms and left me alone in the room. Tears streamed down my face as I again sat there wishing I could trade places with my baby girl. She was perfect and I was broken.

As broken as I was, I needed to start thinking about my three kids at home. I continued to ask about Agnes, but never got a solid answer. Again, I was forced to play the hand I was dealt. You have to be in control of your emotions. If you have a problem controlling your emotions, then you must learn to divert the negative energy to positive energy. One of the amazing things about being a parent is that your children always come first, no matter what.

At this point my family had arrived. I will never forget the scream my sister-in-law let out when she saw me holding Dani. They all wanted to hold her, but when I moved her, I noticed her blood was all over her bottom and on my jeans. My sister got a nurse and they took her to re-stitch the cut in her stomach where they injected her with saline. My mother stayed with me when they took Dani. My sisters and sister-in-law went to check on Agnes.

Agnes held her own in the operating room as she fought for her life, she was a strong woman. My sisters said the doctor gave my wife no comfort as they wheeled her right by him. This just solidified what a classless monster he really was. This guy may have been smart enough to become a doctor, but if jobs were based on compassion, he wouldn't be able to get a job anywhere but the slaughterhouse.

Everyone returned to the room while Agnes was in surgery. Moments later, Dani was brought back in. Everyone took turns holding her as I went to see Agnes.

My wife looked as if the life was drained from her. Pregnancy is taxing enough on a woman when she gets to hold her child in her arms, but its insult to injury when you have to return home with nothing but a painful memory. In the recovery room, I remember her asking if this really happened. She blamed herself. She said she should have known. When I started to console her she told me she had lost her uterus and couldn't have any more children. She was at the bottom of the barrel. She was reaching out for me, needing me more than ever. I just kept telling her we would get through it together, we always had before, and this wouldn't be any different. I couldn't fall apart now; I needed to be there for her.

She was spent on all levels—physically, emotionally, and mentally. When they brought Dani in for Agnes to hold, she held on to her as if she was going to get a lifetime of hugs in that small window of time. I can still see her kissing our little angel's head. More proof that love doesn't die.

Chapter 32

As the head of my family, I kept my composure in the hospital. I focused my mind on anything positive that I could think of to keep my own spirits up. When I was alone, that was a different story. My drive home was extremely hard. Leanne Womack's "I Hope You Dance," came on the radio and tears just started streaming down my face. I kept thinking, *how am I going to break it to the kids about their baby sister? How does this happen in this day and age?* I took a deep breath before entering the house and calling the kids. I just laid everything out for them. It's been said the truth hurts, and it can, but hearing it also immediately starts the healing process.

The kids were upset and confused, almost not knowing how to react. They returned to what they were doing, but in a somber mood. I went up to our room to just lie down for a minute, but right as I started to doze off, the phone rang. Agnes was on the other end. She wondered if I could bring her mother down to the hospital. Physically I didn't think I could, but I couldn't disappoint her. I sat up, gathered myself, and pressed forward.

When my mother-in-law and I arrived back at the hospital, she went to get flowers with my sister, leaving Agnes and me a moment to ourselves. Agnes again began to blame herself. "I wouldn't blame you if you wanted to find someone else," she said to me. "Someone you could have more kids with."

I told her I wasn't going anywhere. That we had a long road ahead of us, but that length would lessen if we traveled it together. Then we shared a kiss that seemed like our first. That made me realize that while my heart was broken, it was far from empty. It felt like we won a battle in a long, drawn out war.

When my mother-in-law and sister returned to the room, I left to be with the kids. I took them to my parent's house so that my mom could make them pancakes for breakfast. The hospital had given me a picture of Dani. My mother had already seen her, so I showed it to my father who hadn't been able to make it to the hospital because it bothered him so much. Trying to keep composed, he said she was beautiful. Then he went into his room. My father and I never made eye contact again for the remaining months he had to live.

The tragedy of Dani's death had a ripple effect on those I loved. I was beginning to feel the effects myself. I was looking at my three children and could only see that I was missing one. I felt like a boxer getting a standing eight count. Do I let the towel be thrown in or do I get back into the fight where I might be knocked out? But I have always believed in the chance of a comeback. I would go out swinging. I couldn't imagine what was going through my children's heads, so we picked up a few of their cousins and went to the batting cages to get our minds off the tragedy.

The ride to the batting cages was silent. My guard was falling. My best effort wasn't good enough; the tears just began to fall. It felt like all eyes were on me. I was the guy they all looked up to, and I was letting them down. I was looking for a spark—someone or something to point me in the right direction. Then my son Billy said, "Dad, when are you going to be fun again?" It was that simple sentence that would springboard me toward recovery. I decided at that moment that I wouldn't let anyone see me grieve. My responsibilities were my wife and the three children I had.

Although I was back on my feet, Agnes was in the hospital reliving every terrible moment. When I visited her that afternoon she asked if I had talked to her sister Mariola and brother-in-law Jeff, who were in Hawaii with their son Andy. I told her I didn't. We then decided to hold off on the news so as to not ruin their good time. Mariola and Jeff often called to check on Agnes to see if she had given birth yet. We needed to be ready for the phone call. Agnes told me I needed to answer the phone because I was the only one who could do it and not break into tears. I remember thinking, *great, my mind is on board, but my heart still isn't up to speed.* But, I was sticking to my guns. I was going to be an example, a pillar of strength for my family.

Later that night our home caller I.D. lit up with an unknown number. It was time to walk the walk. I pulled myself together and picked up the phone. Fortunately for me, my nephew was on the other end. "What's up, jackass?" he said. That was exactly what I needed to hear. That comment put me in the right frame of mind. I was on my game, dodging all the questions about Dani. I simply said Agnes hadn't gone into labor yet, that Agnes and her mother were out shopping. They called two more times that week; both times I answered and kept the news from them.

When Agnes returned from the hospital, we tried to continue out routine prior to our loss as much as we could. My mother-in-law and I put all of the baby clothes away and stored them away from sight. I took the crib down and put the ultra sounds away.

Our best efforts to brighten our house seemed to fall short. There was and always would be something missing. It's a void that can't be replaced, so you need to focus on what you have—an uphill battle to say the least. My advice is love can conquer all and can light your way through any darkness.

The night Mariola and Jeff returned home, I left them a note on their garage door explaining the situation. When you come home from vacation, you just want to relax in your own environment, not visit with anyone, but they drove right over and stayed about two hours offering us their support. Later that night, Agnes told me that her sister had offered to carry a baby for us. This was to become a big issue for us, but for now we put it on the back burner. We had to prepare for Dani's funeral.

The protocol for a child's funeral is to have it at the cemetery, but Agnes wanted to have it at the church. She spoke with one of the younger priests and they talked about having a full Mass. The Father learned that the church wasn't being used on a Saturday morning, and he called Agnes and I and told us he would do a full Mass. It was nice to know there were good people out there and Agnes needed something to go her way.

Friends and family were rallying around us through this awful time. I was hurt, though, when a family member called and told us he had to work and couldn't make the service. I don't know who wouldn't allow a few hours off so an employee could attend a child's funeral. My friend Ron Garney who was an artist for Marvel Comics and has deadlines all the time found the time to make it. I guess it's all about your priorities. Ron's another friend with whom I have been blessed. It seems like I can talk to him about anything, though most of the time we bust on each other. It's always good to laugh, even if you're the brunt of the joke. I am amazed by his creativity, which is only exceeded by his heart.

Even if there was no possibility of getting the time off from work, then at least send someone to represent your family. If money matters more than people, then we're living in a sad world. I thought of this family member like a brother, but when I look back, I realized he was never there when I needed him the most. His insensitivity hurt deeply, but Agnes and I decided never to talk about it again.

Then there was my friend, Cindy. I unthinkingly called and told her what had happened, not taking into consideration that she was expecting a child of her own. I can't tell you how bad I felt after I hung up that phone. She had enough to worry about having her first child without having to worry about the horror we just went through. Two days later I called her, and told her I was sorry. I'll never forget how she responded. "That's just like you," she said. "Worried about someone else instead of yourself." Having your first child is one of the greatest, most exciting moments you can have, so making sure she had what I said in the back of her mind was important to me.

Our daughter's funeral was a great show of support for her and our family. What we thought would be mostly family turned into something much more. Friends and co-workers also joined us to lift our spirits on this difficult day.

Chapter 33

Agnes and I were focusing on our family and on each other. The nurses at the hospital had counseled Anges that most couples break apart after a loss, but I kept reinforcing we weren't most couples.

After the funeral, we started falling back into our routine. Like clockwork, Agnes came down every night at 10:30 and wanted to talk when everyone was sleeping. Most of the time, we would relive the night of Dani's death to the point it would seem real. We eventually told each other about the dreams we both had the night before we went to have Dani. Both of us wondered why we had the dream twenty-four hours before it happened. The only thing that I came up with was that maybe God was preparing us for what was about to happen.

The other subject we grappled with was having another baby. This eventually became a real issue between us.

At first it all seemed like a go. Agnes's sister said she wanted to be the surrogate for us, but at the first day of testing at the doctor's office, her sister got cold feet. This set Agnes back for a while. She didn't understand why her sister would make the offer and then back out. I thought that she meant well, but perhaps she spoke too soon due to the devastating circumstances, not really expecting us to take her up on it. At the time Agnes couldn't see her side of it.

Chapter 33

Agnes was focused on what she lost and wasn't thinking about what she had. She reached a point in her life where she didn't trust more than a few people. I became the person Agnes trusted the most, but even I couldn't get through to her. She would listen but not hear what I was telling her. Physically, she didn't feel like a complete woman, and it was hard for her to gather herself mentally because she had so much weighing on her.

She was dead set on having another child. She would search the Internet and print out different offering surrogacy options. I had promised to try surrogacy, so we pursued the options. Between us we had six sisters, one sister had the ability to carry a child, and she wasn't willing. We needed to find someone outside the family.

The day before Thanksgiving, I ran into a friend from high school. She asked about the family and how we were doing. I told her about our situation. She mentioned that she had always thought about carrying a child for someone. When I got home, Agnes could tell I had something to tell her. I would always start off by saying, "Don't get your hopes up, but we might have someone." But Agnes always latched on to any glimmer of hope. But this hope was again short lived.

When we met with my friend, she said she was okay with it, but her husband was not. There are a lot of variables in this procedure, a lot that needs to go right, if not perfect. Even though we weren't even close to having another child, it was really frustrating to continue a process we were destined to fail. But, things were about to get worse.

Chapter 34

We went to our lawyers to discuss our pending lawsuit against the doctor and hospital in the tragedy of Danielle's death. The lawyers had told us from the get-go that this case was solid. Agnes and I were both eager to get our story out. We didn't want this doctor to do this to any other family ever again.

I also thought the process of the lawsuit would be healing for Agnes. We needed something to go our way to get us to the next stage of grief. However, when it came time for the doctor's deposition, he cancelled saying he was too busy.

Incredibly, we would wait years before the doctor "had time" for his deposition. Between the two doctors in question, the depositions were rescheduled at least ten times in the first two years. Every time they were due to be deposed, we had to relive that nightmare.

It felt like every time Agnes started feeling better, either our lawsuit or the surrogacy issues would bring her right back down.

Like I said, though, there were problems on both fronts. Our surrogate search led us to another woman in Connecticut. We went to her house and went over her demands. I didn't get a good vibe from the get go. This lady wanted $12,000 for the maternity clothes alone. Believe me this is a major commitment and who ever goes through this process should be paid well, but both sides should feel comfortable— and no one needs that many maternity clothes! On our ride home, I threw the ball in Agnes' court. "What did you think?" I asked.

The good thing was, Agnes wasn't impulsive. She thought everything through.

"What do you think?" she asked.

"Does my opinion matter?" I responded. I knew it mattered, but I wanted her to see it was a two-person decision. I wanted Agnes to know that I was in this for the long haul. She needed that reassurance to gather her own strength. She was a very strong woman who had been knocked off her track. It was my job to be her guide, to get her back to that track. We both eventually decided that this surrogate wasn't the right fit. Again we came up empty handed, and were left with nothing but questions.

Agnes may have not been impulsive, but she was tenacious. This was good and bad, depending on the subject. I needed to use that quality in her to help her heal from the loss of Dani. My motto was, Time heals, but why wait? Life is too short with no guarantees, so the faster you can get yourself back on track the better served you will be. The only problem is that all people heal at different speeds. Danielle's death killed me, but with Agnes turning to me for strength I had no choice but to heal. I always wondered if I reversed the roles on her, would she rise to the occasion and be that rock for me? The only reason I didn't try this tactic was because she was too smart to fall for it.

Chapter 35

The doctors continued to cancel their depositions and Agnes continued to search for another surrogate. Then she found this woman who lived in the next town. At first I thought she was a good person. She said she was a single mom and wanted to be a surrogate to put her daughter through college. She would call or email Agnes every day. She also did her homework on the procedures from start to finish. At this point, she seemed like the right fit. We went to the initial doctor's visit to see if she was physically able to carry a child. We got the green light, and although it was nice to see Agnes smile, I started to have reservations. I decided to keep them to myself, though, as I didn't want to take the wind out of Agnes's sails.

The next day, Agnes came home for lunch and told me that this surrogate wanted us to sign the contract because her daughter was going to college and she wanted to make a payment. We had yet to determine if she was mentally competent, but Agnes wanted to roll the dice. I wanted to say no, but Agnes was a great judge of character. Who was I to take this dream away from her?

Agnes was so excited. She was so looking forward to our new child. She would tell me it was going to be a girl, and we were going to name her Faith. I'm a very positive person, but all of the sudden I couldn't have anything but negative thoughts about bringing another child into the world.

For the next few days I kept to myself, trying to find the positive in the situation, but that Saturday when we showed up at the surrogate's house with $3,000, she and I seemed to be at odds—and it wasn't all me. She noticed me looking at her arms; she always wore long sleeves. She also drank a lot of tea and I took interest in which ones she was drinking. Regardless of everything my gut was telling me, we signed the contract, and she got her money. I continued to keep my thoughts to myself, hoping and praying I was wrong.

The following week, I went in to a local GNC to inquire about the tea I had seen at the surrogate's house. I understood there are many benefits of drinking herbal teas, but what I didn't know and what the woman from the store told me was that they can be used to mask drugs. I was at a crossroads. I wanted Agnes to receive this gift of life, but not at the expense of our child. I knew I needed more than a feeling to convince my wife this might not be the right choice. I prayed that God would give me the wisdom, strength, anything to make the right moves, and then I got my answer at the next doctor's appointment.

The surrogate went in for and passed the mental evaluation, but the doctors had their reservations. The surrogate looked like a deer in the headlights, and Agnes picked up on it immediately. We met with the nurse who asked us if we were sure about our surrogate choice. As I voiced my opinion, I could see almost all hope leave Agnes. Still nothing was said to the surrogate on our ride home and we went on with the process. Without question Agnes was hurt, left again to question why.

"I've said so many prayers," she told me. "Why would this happen?"

"I think God wants us to start appreciating what we have," I said gently. I could see the writing on the wall, but it was so difficult to see her so hurt again.

Her new goal as well as her heart was now shattered again. Agnes blamed herself for what happened. She threw everything on herself, from the emotions we had to experience to the money we lost. She felt as if she had cheated the kids and me. I tried to assure her that she would have been cheating herself if she hadn't tried for another baby. "We've seen worse days," I told her. "The real tragedy would have been if she gave birth to a sick or ill baby because of her addiction."

In my heart, I knew that this was a blessing; I just needed to get Agnes to see that. I kept telling her things happen for reasons, but that wasn't an easy sell.

We still needed to be sure, there still was the possibility we were wrong about the surrogate. So we (with the nurse's help) set up another appointment. We told the surrogate that they were just going to go over all the procedures so everybody was clear on what and when to expect things. This way she wasn't expecting a test and so wouldn't think of masking her drug use.

At the appointment, the nurse brought in a cup and told the surrogate she'd need to take a drug test. The look on her face said it all. She was caught off guard; her gig was up. She went into that bathroom two to three times, every time saying she couldn't pee. The nurse brought her out water, about a half gallon. When she was finally able to provide a sample, she diluted it with water. Agnes needed to see no more.

A good mother never puts her children in harm's way. And Agnes was a great mom! Life's lessons aren't always easy, and people can be mean and deceitful. We didn't get what we wanted, but we also didn't wind up with something we didn't deserve. We were back to picking up the pieces, but this time we wanted to make it right. We both thought it wasn't just about making our lives right, but others around us.

Chapter 36

Our feelings toward the doctor we had on that fateful night in the hospital with Dani were so strong that we decided we were going to go after his medical license. At first our lawyers were against it because it would interfere with the lawsuit, but we weren't backing down. Our lawyers were the best, and this guy couldn't be any guiltier. It was no longer about money; it was about doing what was right. If we could do anything about it, this monster wasn't going to affect another life the way he changed ours.

We filed the papers, and the ball was rolling. But, just like all the other processes, this one would take a while. For what it was worth, it was nice to think maybe he was having a sleepless night or two. He might be able to prolong things for a while, but his day would come.

Agnes wanted to get some professional help. She felt ashamed to tell me, as if in some way she was letting me down. She was scraping the bottom of the barrel, and only a few things could bring her pleasure. This was a sure sign of depression and she was a strong woman for admitting it.

To her credit she never let the kids see her hurting. She was the ultimate mother and wife. It was only at night that she would let her guard down and really allow her emotions to show.

She started counseling and I was able to go to all but one session for her. I think it's very important to show any person making that step to get herself better, that you're in her corner. I remember one time when I was sitting next to her and she took my hand. Words can't describe the connection we had at that moment.

She felt very comfortable with her doctor, and that's important for the healing process. The doctor prescribed her medicine, which at first Agnes was against, but this was the best solution to the problem.

We would still talk every night and things went on as usual, except for our workouts. We had some equipment in the basement and we started working out together. We pushed each other to get better. The workouts made us physically stronger, but they also relieved our stress.

We had three kids and not a whole lot of time to work with, but every night after we put them to bed we headed to our "gym." The first two weeks were rough, you're tired and it's hard to get motivated, but the workouts will change your metabolism. They allow your body to require less rest. The workouts definitely changed our outlooks, it couldn't have been more than a month before you could feel and see the results.

One of the steps the doctor wanted Agnes to take was to put away the clothes we had for Danielle. Although it was very hard for her, she did it. We were starting to win battles, gain the ground we needed. We also started to make changes to our house, change the environment around us. A new start turned out to be very refreshing, and the time we spent on planning and accomplishing our goals kept our minds from our grief.

Agnes also grew very close and was very involved in our children's lives. She would never miss a game or school conference. She sat down with the kids every night to do their homework, and, no matter how late it was, she would make them something to eat if they were hungry. She was starting to refocus her energy from negative to positive. I started keeping track of her good days and bad days. After two months, I showed her the progress she was making, how she could string together three or four good days in a week. Some weeks had five or six days. I wanted to show her that she could smile again, have good times again. That one bad day didn't dictate a bad week. That one bad week didn't dictate a bad month or a bad month dictate a bad year? To some, a bad day may look like a mountain in your path, but I saw a speed bump. A mountain is a hard obstacle to climb or move, a speed bump may slow you down, but it allows you to continue forward.

During one of Agnes's therapy sessions she told the doctor that I was her strength. She didn't know how I could wake up every day with a smile on my face. To say that was a bittersweet moment was an understatement. On one hand, I knew I meant everything to her; on the other hand, I was at a place she wanted to be. I continued to give Agnes positive reinforcement and prayed that I could keep on my path and not crash. Only God knows what tomorrow might bring, so I prepared to cross whatever bridge he chose for me.

Chapter 37

Since the doctors continued to delay proceedings in our lawsuit, we requested to do our depositions first, to get the ball rolling. We were both tired of turning the other cheek. It was time to put pressure on them.

On July 17, 2003, Agnes had her deposition. She wasn't nervous at all, she was just happy to tell our side of the story. It's not like this guy just made a mistake that awful night. We knew he had questionable service prior to that night, and his reaction to us after the fact was what spurred us to bring a suit in the first place.

I was so proud of Agnes that day. Maybe it was a mother's love for her child, but Agnes had so much strength and composure. It seemed our little angel was on her shoulder that day. The lawyers' best efforts were kept at bay. Agnes used her anger to give herself strength, instead of letting it cloud her judgment or her actions.

Then it was my turn. Agnes was so gun-ho on the goal that she wanted to start grilling me with questions. I could have used the prep, but I didn't want to overexpose the nightmares of that night to her. She was getting better, and I didn't want to set her back. I knew what was coming, what to expect, I just wanted to get it done.

The only way I could prepare myself was to face my emotions. The nights before my deposition, I would make sure Agnes was sleeping. Then I would go downstairs and put myself through the worst moments of that night. I would spend a half hour beating myself up, then forty-five minutes or so trying to calm myself down. So many people had told me, "You have strong shoulders." What good are strong shoulders when you have an empty heart? I kept telling myself I was her father and now I needed to be her voice.

The thought of that doctor made my skin crawl. Many times he came into where I worked. I worked at a sporting goods store. He'd walk around me, wanting me to hit him. I would go in the back, take a few deep breaths, and then I would ask God for the strength to do the right thing. I thank God for keeping me from sinking to this idiot's level, and keeping me on the right track. In this life it might not be the most rewarding thing, but I'll take my chances in the after life.

This doctor is a monster without a soul, but he was also a husband and a father. Although I didn't have the greatest faith in our legal system, I didn't see any other way to get justice. Cooler heads prevail, that's true. After Dani died, there were many times I came in contact with this so-called doctor. And, every time I had visions of ruining his world. That would have been a selfish, easy situation for me—for me only. My family was already devastated; I couldn't do it to them again. Everything we had done to recover would be for nothing. We had no choice but to continue to rely on the legal system.

Finally, the day of my deposition was here. I was as ready as I could be. I had been in this position before, oddly enough, against the same lawyer once before. I guess he didn't mind representing the wrong. As they had with Agnes, they started off with the pleasant questions before pouncing and trying to trip me up. Agnes was by my side, and it meant a lot knowing how painful it was for her to sit there and have to relive that night—again. She gave me so much strength.

One of the defense attorneys was a female, most likely a mother herself. My description of that night brought her to tears. Our lawyer told us later that it was a great sign that the lawyer for the other side was moved to tears. He said, "If she tears up during the testimony, then so would a jury." I wasn't looking for sympathy, but I would take that route if it meant I could stop this man from delivering babies.

I didn't like the way my deposition was going with them always on the attack. I decided to turn the tables on them by dropping the bombshell that we were going after the doctor's medical license. The opposing lawyers switched gears immediately, trying to get as much information out of me while I was under oath. I had planned this all along; I was just waiting for the right moment. It was the doctor's turn for some sleepless nights.

Chapter 38

The summer went by quickly and for the most part was uneventful. Before we knew it, it was Thanksgiving. Agnes was still not talking with her sister. But as I've learned, God usually has other plans for people than they have for themselves. My brother-in-law's mother died and Agnes and I went to the funeral. Even though Mariola and Agnes only exchanged small talk, the ice was broken. I really wanted Agnes and her sister to resolve things, so that Saturday I asked Agnes if she would talk to her sister if Mariola called. She said she would, so I did the next best thing and called her sister. The two talked for a good amount of time to catch up for lost time. Things seemed as though they were getting back to normal—at least on that front.

Chapter 39

The lawsuit, not so much. We were again short-changed by the doctors as they cancelled on us that next week. We met with our lawyers and set a plan in motion. That night, we stopped by my parents' house and my father tried to comfort Agnes by telling her to stick to her guns. Unfortunately, that was the last advice he would ever give to her. The next day, December 12, 2001, my father passed away.

The morning of December 12, I had a doctor's appointment. My dad had a large pile of wood that needed stacking, so I told him that we should do it that afternoon. I picked the kids up from school and went to his house. We went to my Dad's but we couldn't find him. We looked around the yard for him, but came up empty. My grandmother's house was across the street, so I thought he might be over there.

As I walked to my grandmother's house, I noticed the bathroom light was on in my parent's bathroom, and then heard their dog howling. I ran back to the house. As soon as I stepped into their bedroom, I got that empty feeling in my chest again. When I entered the bathroom, I noticed his leg on the ground. As I turned the corner, I saw that he was half in the tub and half on the floor. I tried to feel for a pulse, but did not get one. I ran to the phone to call 911. I gave them the address and told them I was going to start C.P.R.

But, when I returned to the bathroom I noticed how stiff my dad was. I knew he was gone. I took a moment to thank him for being a great father and all the things he taught me and gave me. Then I had to focus on my mother; she was the one with the bad heart.

When I went back to the kitchen to call 911 again, I told the dispatcher that my father was dead. They were on their way, so I then left a message on Agnes' voicemail. I then got in touch with my sisters Jen and Maryanne. Jen did not take the news well at all, so I had my sister Maryanne pick her up.

When my mom came into the house I told her to sit down to tell her the bad news. Moments later, the emergency workers showed up and they looked over my mother while another fireman went into the bathroom to help my father. My father hated going to the hospital or doctors' offices, but he loved life too much not to fight for it. When I exited the bathroom, I noticed a bottle of holy water and a prayer card on my father's bed. Maybe he had known what was coming. Agnes and my other sisters arrived shortly after the EMTs. We were all shocked with no answers.

Late that night I was staring out our bedroom window when Agnes rubbed my head and told me to come to bed. She kept her arm around me and said, "I am right here; wake me up if you need me."

There are two ways this could have gone. If I did fall, maybe she would have risen to the occasion and set me back on my feet. Or, she could have fallen back, thinking maybe I wasn't everything she thought I was. I missed my father, but I couldn't forget what he taught me, the person he helped me build. He would have wanted me to be strong for my family, just like he was all those years for my mother, sisters, and me.

At my father's wake, Agnes and I were praying as we knelt by his casket. When we stood up, Agnes said, "You are running out of time." I was confused at first, until she told me to give my father a kiss. My father and I had a different type of relationship; we knew what we both meant to each other so we did not need to reinforce it in other ways, but I took her advice and kissed him on the forehead for the first and last time.

The number of people my father had touched amazed me. For forty-eight hours, I recalled a lot of good times we had. I was asked to give the eulogy, so I wrote it out by points so I wouldn't lose focus. One point I made was how I felt that the torch now passed on to me. I didn't want it, nor was I ready for it, but there was no going back. Some things you can't prepare for, you just have to cross that bridge when you come to it. Is what's on the other side of that bridge better? Sometimes no, but it will be what you make of it.

My father constantly talked about how great life was. He would be the last one to want people to suffer from his death. I could have talked for days about what my father meant to me, gave me, or taught me, but he would have told me to look back on a life, look back on the lessons, but leave the loss behind you.

My dad always enjoyed a good laugh. I know he enjoyed this one. When I stepped away from the podium and started down the stairs, I hit the second stair wrong on my slippery shoes, and went air borne. The sound of the impact made an echo throughout the church. I looked at it as my father's way of putting a smile on everybody's face. I can't tell you how fast I sprung up—as if nobody would have seen me! When I got back to Agnes, she said, "I meant to tell you the bottom of your shoes were slick." I asked her if she laughed. "Yeah," she said. "Once I knew you were okay."

Outside the church, everybody pretty much said the same thing, and they were all smiling. Those smiles gave me the reassurance that good times would come sooner than later.

After paying our respects to my dad at the cemetery, we stopped one more time to pray. That night, although she hesitated, Agnes confided that she was happy that Danielle wouldn't be alone in heaven anymore. She didn't mean it in a bad way. She wasn't happy my dad was gone, but she was happy that he could look after Dani for us now. She rubbed my head until I fell asleep.

The next day was something I will never forget. It started like any other day, but then I noticed Agnes watching me intently a few times. After about an hour, she asked, "How is it that you can smile?"

I told her I feel like it's a waste of life to mope around and not look at every moment as a blessing. Nobody but God knows what tomorrow will bring, so I think we need to take and make the most of what we do have.

I kept hearing people say they wished they could have one more day with my dad, or that one last chance to say, "I love you." It's funny the things we take for granted until they are no longer there.

Chapter 40

Less then two weeks later it was Christmas. My father used to go to great lengths to plan and put on the holiday dinners; he enjoyed doing for others. The holidays were different now, but still special in their own ways. I remember my sister Maryanne saying, "I can't believe I am forty years old and lost my father." I responded by telling her she had had him for ten years longer than I did. I wasn't trying to get sympathy; I just wanted her to see it could be worse.

The last thing I wanted to do was find my father dead, but if anyone had to do it, I'm glad it was me. I already faced my darkest day, and was now stronger then I ever thought I could be.

My father and I had set up the Christmas lights for my house for what turned out to be the last time. Agnes and I would always take them down a week or so after New Year's. This year was different though. Agnes never said anything; she waited for me to make the first move. She didn't know if I was going to leave them up. And she didn't want to be the one to tell me to take them down. We eventually took them down. I realized you always have your memories to hold on to.

Agnes looked at me differently after the day my father died. She told me I was always bigger than any problem. This wasn't true. I needed to somehow show her that it wasn't me; it was the two of us together. We were together in all aspects of life, and together, I felt we could take on anything.

Agnes was still thinking about what was said to her at the hospital when Danielle died. They had told her that a 90 percent of couples break up after such a loss. This was a terrible seed to plant at such a vulnerable time. Agnes felt a distance between us because that thought kept looming in the back of her mind. Convincing her that we were going to beat the odds was a difficult task.

The loss of my father reignited Agnes's passion for a bigger family. Physically, Agnes wasn't feeling like the woman she wanted to be. Not being able to carry any more children really bothered her. Telling her that it didn't matter didn't reassure her although I did it often. She was grasping for straws to try and get back what she had lost. At one point she even bought a pregnancy test because her stomach wasn't its normal flat self. When the test came up negative, she immediately got mad at herself for wasting $30. It seemed like she wanted me to be mad at her, too. Was I? Absolutely not, how do you get mad at someone who just keeps trying? Just keeps giving everything they have? Besides I didn't have time to be mad. I needed to prove to her there were new things that could and would make her happy.

We changed things up a little with our house both inside and out. It kept us busy, our minds on a new goal. My father used to do a majority of landscaping, but now that fell to me. Agnes asked if that bothered me. I told her yes, but only because I couldn't get the yard to look half as nice as he had. When I was doing something wrong, I could hear my father's voice echoing the lessons he had taught me all those years. That voice faded with each day, though. The best way I could explain it was that the people I've lost were in my heart more than they were in my head.

Because of what I had been through, I was never allowed to grieve. I became more of a counselor for others. I guess "been there, done that" is how they looked at it. In their eyes I was bulletproof; it wasn't that I didn't hurt; I just heal quicker then most. It's said that there's always someone who has it worse than you do; that's who I feel sorry for. So far I had lived up to how others perceived me, especially Agnes.

Agnes and I took everyday as it came, facing things as we encountered them. She was gaining ground with her recovery, and that's important to point out. She was making notes of her progress and setting new goals. She began not to limit herself. She did a little extra every day just to give herself that edge. To recover fast, you have to learn not to settle for the progress you've made. It was important for her to have her mind as an ally and not as the enemy. She had been so busy beating herself up for things that were not her fault. It was time for her to realize that.

Chapter 41

The time had finally come, when the doctor's days of ducking his deposition were over. We arrived early at the hospital's lawyer's office in New Haven for the deposition. Agnes kept squeezing my hand under the table as her breaths became more rapid and shallow. "Aren't you nervous?" she asked: I told her there was nothing wrong with nerves, she just needed to let them feed her anger. She told me that she didn't know if she could even look at the doctor. I told her to look past him, focus on something behind him, but stare in his direction. I wanted him to think she was stronger now and he wouldn't be able to intimidate her anymore.

His stance was that he was in the driver's seat. So far he had everything but the suit itself going his way. He walked into the room as if he was untouchable—smiling, cocky, and confident.

He and I only made eye contact twice, as he focused most of his attention Agnes. He came right out of the gates lying and infuriating her. She kept her composure until we broke for the lunch break. She told our lawyer, "He's lying"! Our lawyer assured her not to worry because it was apparent that he was lying. He denied or couldn't recall anything that happened that night. I was mad because he had waited so long that now he could just say he couldn't remember. I know he couldn't change the outcome, but he was making it seem like my daughter's had been an accident.

Our lawyers didn't fire all their guns at once, so their questions weren't very revealing or hard on him. I imagine the doctor left that office that day thinking he gained ground. Things are not always how they appear.

The doctor wasn't as important that day as Agnes and how she did. She walked in a victim with a head of negativity, unable to stand for herself, and walked out stronger, more confident woman. That was her point of no return. She would no longer leave me to stand by myself when it came to our daughter. It comes a lot easier than you think, changing those crippling thoughts into a fire that charges you full steam ahead.

As soon as we got home she called the state's attorney's office to see how far along the process was in revoking his medical license. They were still reviewing the charts and notes on the case and didn't have a clear indication on when it would be finished. But the day was coming, and that's all we wanted to know. She began to organize and add to the file. Her outlook, her demeanor, had turned around completely. She began to take life as it came, facing the good with the bad. She still came down to talk with me every night, but it wasn't about the bad moments as much. It did still come up from time to time, but not every night like it had before.

She also became very close to God. She had always believed and been a good Catholic, but now it was in her soul. Little things, special moments had so much meaning to her. She began to carry herself without the aid of others or medicine. She began to arrange her life in the way she needed it. Her heart was always in the right place, but now her head was moving in the right direction, too. She was beginning to restore herself to where she could leave her demons in the past.

It finally clicked for her and she apologized to me for not being able to grieve with me. I had three sleepless nights between Dani's death and her funeral. Everything in the house seemed so quiet, and I kept hearing a child's footsteps running across the wood floors. It was a helpless feeling for me knowing I couldn't save her. Agnes asked me how I stopped those negative thoughts after the third day. I told her I made a conscious decision that Danielle would always be in my heart and only in my head when I needed the memories.

As Agnes started to feel better mentally, she threw herself into her workouts. Even if it was only for fifteen minutes a day, we were in the weight room. She would tell me I forgot what it was like to workout hard. I told her if I had forgotten I would probably be down there more often.

Getting back into shape isn't the easiest, but after two or three weeks you can start to see the dividends. It's important to have pride in yourself, to have some self worth. In sports or training you get more results by pushing yourself. The healing process has its restrictions, but you achieve goals when you put in the effort. Agnes was living life again, focusing on the moment. It was a matter of losing in order to gain an appreciation of life. She had realized she wasn't going to get anywhere by keeping her mind stuck on that one bad day. She woke up everyday now with a positive outlook, with a world of energy. Everyday she had something she wanted to get done, something to accomplish. Our house had never looked so good, both inside and out. Agnes had a great work ethic, so I knew once she was on the road to recovery she would be fine.

Chapter 42

Part 5

July 1, 2005

On Friday July 1, 2005, I went downstairs for breakfast. Agnes was cooking and showing no signs of any problems. She even said nothing was wrong when I asked her. After breakfast I took a shower as she made my lunch for work. When I came down, she handed me my lunch and a bottle of Tang, gave me a kiss, and told me to have a good day. I never would have thought a peck on the lips would have meant so much, but that was to be the last kiss we would share together.

Agnes had doctors appointments scheduled for the kids and her mother, so she was out and about all day. When I got home, I ate dinner with my son Billy and then we were off to his All-Star game. Agnes had our daughter Casey when she picked up my mother for the baseball game.

They arrived about ten minutes before the start of the game. She handed my mother one of the folding chairs and I took hers and began to open it when she grabbed my arm. I thought that she was having an anxiety attack so I told her, "It's okay." She told me to call 911. As I was dialing, she grabbed my mother's hand, then my hand, too. Agnes then dropped to a knee. I continued to tell her to relax and to calm down. For me it was one of those moments where I felt like I was speaking over my heartbeats. Tunnel vision of focus is how I'd best explain it.

People rushed to Agnes's aid. At this point she had to lie on the grass. I kept telling myself; *it's going to be okay.* If she were going to die, it would've happened the night that Dani left us.

A woman who happened to be a nurse kept trying to communicate with Agnes, only to get a long, drawn-out, "Wh-a-a-a-a-t." Then we noticed that Agnes was beginning to have a face drop. I immediately thought that she was having a stroke. Then everything went black, I was out on my feet. I somehow got a second wind and adrenaline must have kicked in. The ambulance along with a police officer arrived. I brought our things to the mini-van and waited to follow.

This is the part, if any, that I would change. If I could go back, I would have ridden in the ambulance with her, but that is the price of being so optimistic. To me, it was unthinkable that I could lose her. This wasn't her time. The ambulance rushed to the hospital and I was right behind it, but it felt like it took a lifetime to get there.

I wish insurance cards were like credit cards, that you could just swipe them and it would give the hospital all the needed information. Because of the time I wasted giving information to the nurses' station, I lost my chance to have any final words with my wife.

When I entered the room, that feeling that I experienced all too often came over me again. I walked in knowing she was gone. The nurse told me to talk to her; maybe it would make a difference. I knew better: I knew she had crossed over. I told her if she needed to go with Danielle, then somehow I would take care of Billy, Jeremy, and Casey. I also thanked her for the time we spent together. Although we only had such a limited amount together, I wouldn't have changed one second of it for anything.

The doctor then came into ask me if I knew if Agnes might have taken any drugs that afternoon. The funny thing was, I almost wanted it to be drugs, because then they could fix her. When I told the doctor that it wasn't drugs, he started telling me how bad things were. He was using a lot of technical terms, things I didn't want to hear. I had him call my sister Mo, the nurse, and explain to her. Mo straight up told me that the situation was bad, and that the family was on their way. At this point they believed Agnes was suffering from an aneurysm. They were right.

They brought me into a room while Agnes was taken down for X rays. The room was just so quiet and I was trying to figure out a plan. A hospital worker came in to talk to me about the situation. She wondered how I was doing. I simply told her the only thing that was on my mind were my three kids.

I also thanked God for the timing. Only moments before she collapsed, she had been driving with our daughter Casey and my mother. If she had collapsed sooner, there was no telling what could have happened.

At this point I received a call from Father Charlie, our priest. He said he didn't know where the hospital was located, but he would be there as soon as he could.

The first relatives to arrive were my in-laws, Jeff, Mariola, and my nephew Andy. We sat there crying. I remember saying, "I don't think she's coming back."

"She's a strong kid," Jeff tried to assure me. "Don't count her out."

This had nothing to do with strength; it was all about heart, and I knew where her heart was. There wasn't a lot of talking after that. I sat there wondering how I was going to explain to my kids that their mother might not make it.

It wasn't long after that, that they arrived at the hospital—three children all-waiting for a miracle. We all went in to see her before they prepped her for surgery. Although they differed in age, all three children walked into that room realizing how fragile life really was. They were all thinking of what they had just twenty-four hours earlier. As we walked into the hall, we noticed that Father Charlie had arrived. He offered the children and I all the support he could before going in to see Agnes.

The next couple of hours were spent waiting to see how the operation would go. I spent a good hour in the chapel praying. It was a little past 3:00 p.m. when the surgeon came out. He said the surgery had gone well, but that Agnes wasn't out of the woods yet.

We all went home optimistic that she was going to pull through. When we got home, my son Jeremy said, "Dad, is Mom going to be all right?"

I wanted to say yes and let him have a good night's sleep, but I also didn't want him to have false hope. The only words that made sense for me to say were, "She's got a good chance."

That night as I went to bed, I couldn't help but think of the empty space in the bed next to me. Although in my mind I couldn't stop thinking if Agnes or God had prepared me for this. There were about a week's worth of nights that Agnes spent with me in our bed since the death of Danielle. She spent most of the nights sleeping in my daughter Casey's room. I asked God again for strength before finally falling asleep that night.

The next morning we got up, ate breakfast, and headed to the hospital. Over the night, the nurse said that Agnes had made some slight improvement. Her vital signs were improving and she had squeezed the nurse's finger on request. I was upset with myself; my brother-in-law had been right, how could I have counted her out. The surgeon came in and was very pleased by her progress.

Over the span of the next four hours she had to go through a battery of tests. A doctor, who would be performing a majority of the tests asked me to join him in another room to talk in private. He didn't want my family to make my decision for me, so he wanted to ask me alone. He asked me if I would allow students to perform the tests as he watched over them. At this point, I doubted my own judgment. I told him I wanted him to perform all the procedures. I know there is only one way really to learn how to perform these procedures, but I didn't want them to learn on Agnes. I told him she's thirty-three years old; if she were sixty-three, I wouldn't think twice. Right or wrong, I needed his timing and precision to give her the best fighting chance possible. I know he wasn't happy, but he wasn't in my shoes, and I needed to put my family first.

At this point Agnes was gaining ground and even he couldn't tell me otherwise. Things were looking good, but that was about to change.

That afternoon, Agnes suffered a heart attack and required a stint to help her heart function. Agnes was in top physical condition with a very strong heart, so this didn't make any sense to us. The doctors told us if she did recover, she would need a heart transplant within three years. Things went south quickly after that.

I wanted to take some of the stress off the kids, so that night we went to see the town's fireworks. The irony of it being Independence Day was not lost on me. The fireworks were going off, but I was looking past them, toward the sky. Then I looked at my children. I just prayed that they would be all right.

That night, when I took the dogs for a walk, our chocolate lab Duke kept rubbing his paw against my leg. It made me recall the night that Agnes and I had picked him out. A lot of moments ran through my head that night.

My mother called that night around 11:00 p.m. We had a short conversation, but I told her that the next day was going to be the day we found out what direction we would go in. I fell asleep to the good memories, hoping and praying we could make more.

The next morning the phone, instead of my alarm, woke me up. It was 6:36 a.m. Sunday, July 3. I'll never forget it. It was the surgeon saying that Agnes's brain had shut down and only the machines were keeping her alive. He explained it like a fuse box without a fuse. He was a good doctor; you could tell in his voice that he didn't want to make that call. I thanked him for trying his best.

I sat up in bed and wondered if the call was just a dream. I even checked the caller I.D., I knew you couldn't read in a dream. There it was staring right back in my face. I then took down our daughter's keepsake box. As I held Danielle's bag of hair, I asked myself if Agnes was with our angel.

Before I took a shower I read, "Footprints," and asked God to keep my children in mind. I made some calls to family and friends, and gave them the bad news. Everybody showed up to the hospital to say his or her goodbyes that day. Our hope was lost and now in healing mode.

Agnes was an organ donor, so there wasn't just the process of pulling her off the machines. They had to take her off the machines, declare her dead, and then put the machines back on to preserve the organs and tissues. I didn't want to be in the room when they disconnected the machines, but my sister Mo thought I should so that I would never have any doubts. I remember them running a Q-tip over her pupil a few times. Then they flushed water into her ear canal and without the aid of the machines she didn't have any vital signs. Those were some hard words to hear when they called her time of death. It was a stressful ten minutes to see her go through those tests, and then hear those words.

When I walked out of Agnes's room, the donor representatives approached me. Timing may be of the essence in some cases, so you have to think of someone else at this time. Your life is upside-down when you lose someone, but someone else in this time is waiting for the gift of life. The donor people were very professional and knew how to handle the situation. There are lots of difficult and personal, but necessary questions that need to be answered. At the time I didn't realize how important it was, but it wasn't long until I knew differently. My sister and I answered all of their questions as another representative of the donor program gave my kids blankets, butterfly pins, and other keepsakes to take the gravity of the situation off their minds for a moment or two.

When we left the hospital there was a lot of questions to be answered, some in the coming days and some in the distant future. When I put the key into the door as we got home, Billy's voice cracked as he said, "This isn't fair!"

What do you say to a child that could make any sense? I was looking for anything to say to give my kids even the slightest amount of comfort. Your home is supposed to be your safe haven, your comfort zone, but in this case it was a constant reminder of Agnes. Every room in the house held a reminder of a time or moment. That night, before Billy went to bed, he asked me to call the hospital and get the hospital bracelet that Agnes had been wearing. I called the nurses station and two days later, that bracelet arrived in the mail. Sometimes it's the little things that can have so much meaning.

The kids were exhausted and went to bed early that night. Downstairs sitting on my couch like every other night, I looked up toward the stairs every time the house would settle. I just wanted to wake up from this nightmare and see Agnes coming down those stairs. I thought that I needed to focus on the truth, so I began to write down what I would say about Agnes at church. I wrote down the story of her life, the people that she helped, the things she was most proud of, and the place she would now call home. I could have written for a week, but I decided to go to bed at midnight. I did that because it was a new day; it needed to be a new start. I prayed that night that God would give me the strength to help my kids get through this.

Again I couldn't help but wonder if in someway God hadn't prepared me for this moment as I lay in the bed alone. I felt like everything was on me—my children, my family were all pulling for me to endure once again. If you have had a good experience at a funeral home before (that must be an oxymoron), what I mean by this is if you have had a funeral home handle the loss of a loved one in a comforting, professional way, it helps.

The amount of support, cards, food, flowers, and love I received was amazing. My children's friends called or came to play with my kids to take their minds off their loss for the time being.

I tried repeatedly to finish the eulogy for Agnes. Time seemed to be traveling at light speed, and the wake was upon us. I kept waiting for Agnes to bring in my ironed shirt, or help me put my sock on. Everybody's different, but physical pain is so much easier to deal with than emotional. I got caught up thinking to myself this is really happening as I looked at her closet doors closed shut; the usual five different outfits that she couldn't choose between weren't sprawled across the bed. Even right before I went into the funeral home, I got out of the car and called her name. I still don't know why. The whole thing went by like a blur.

After the wake, the kids went to bed without any problems and I continued on her story. We had had so many good times together; I didn't know when or where to stop. It was close to 1:00 a.m. when I stopped writing. There was a lot, but she meant a lot.

The morning came quick after a sleepless night. The last thing that I wanted to be for my kids was a failure. I wanted to be a pillar of strength for them. I made a list to make sure that I wouldn't forget anything. Seconds after I put my pants on; I put the eulogy speech in my pocket. Something about that moment made me think back on all the times that she was there to pick me up and give me support.

The family arrived at the funeral home to pay their last respects. My mother in law used every last moment with her. Everybody was in his or her cars waiting to go the church when I got to see her for the last time. I thanked her for every moment we shared. Although some of those times weren't the best, together we found a way to become more than we were alone. I told her that I was sorry; sorry for the things that we always wanted to do later on in life that we'd never get to do. I then stood over her and let one of my tears fall on her cheek. I kissed her on the tear and told her goodbye.

When we entered the church, I was overwhelmed by the amount of people who were there. I kept thinking about her. I can't tell you much about the Mass other than me kissing my hand and laying it on the casket as I went to read the eulogy. When I got to the podium, I looked at our kids, and thought it is time to be the person I knew I could be. That's the same moment that I held onto the podium and let the words come from my heart rather from the paper I had written. Everyone said later that I did great, but I felt like I maybe didn't do so well.

If actions truly speak louder than words, then I could hear her voice, "Come on, will you get in this picture?" I always took pictures of Agnes and the kids. Talk about priceless; you can't put a monetary value on that. It also makes me wonder if that was because God had known about this plan all along. It's not one of your better days when you have to bury a loved one, especially when they are younger than you. We had so much invested in each other, and now I was going to have to take this stand alone.

My mind was filled with all the doubt in the world as the Priest finished his ceremony at the cemetery. I couldn't think of myself, though, with my children standing there living their worst nightmare. We gathered some of the flowers from the arrangements so that we could save them. After the cemetery, we gathered at my sister's house and I watched as my kids were able to forget the pain for a while and just play. It's amazing how resilient children can be.

Again I had a lot of people pulling for me, wanting me to rise above and becoming an example. Before going home, the children and I returned to the cemetery to say a few more prayers and take a few more flowers. When truly bad things happen, it's amazing how kindhearted people can be. There were more dinners, flowers, and fruit baskets sent. I don't know if it was the stress of the day, but there wasn't a sleepless night for any of us.

The next day we all got up and started an unwelcome, but new chapter in our lives. I was off from work and I thought the best thing I could do was show the kids that life has its moments, but it could be fun again. From the moment they woke up until the second they went to bed, I tried to keep a smile not only on their faces, but on mine as well. We did. However, there was a decision to make. Every year we went to Cape Cod in July. This was Agnes's vacation. She loved the beaches, the restaurants, and everything about the Cape. I didn't know if this was too much, too soon for the kids. Dr. Doug Macgregor, the kids' pediatrician, gave me an answer that made all the sense in the world. "They can be home with painful memories, or they can be at the Cape with painful memories, but at least at the Cape their cousins can keep their minds off those memories for a while." The old formula of winning battles, gaining good days, applied again.

It was a very necessary vacation. The first year without someone always brings the first vacation, the first holidays, the first birthdays. Is it ever easy? Not at all, but the quicker you can get back to the routine, the better you'll be. The kids seemed to have a good time, but for me it wasn't the same. I'm not a big fan of the beach; I always went for the family. The one good thing was that we laughed, and you can't put a premium on laughter. I couldn't help but wonder, though, when we got back home and the laughter stopped, which child would crash first.

Chapter 43

Both boys had made the all-star baseball teams, Billy had no desire to play baseball anymore that summer, but Jeremy wanted to go back and play. The team was great and welcomed him back with open arms. He wore wristbands with his mother's initials, A.Z.G. on them. They also wore memorial decals on their helmets to honor her.

His first game back Jeremy didn't get a hit, but he was hit by two pitches and walked once. I don't know if he noticed or not, but the people in the stands cheered for him, from both sides.

One night, his team was playing to get into the championships. Our team was up by two runs in the fifth inning. Jeremy was playing centerfield. There were two outs but the bases were loaded. The ball was hit hard into centerfield. Jeremy broke for the ball, but it didn't look like he would catch up to it. At the last moment he jumped up and caught the ball. The crowd gave him a standing ovation.

He ran off that field and right to me. He was beaming when he told me that while he was standing in the outfield there was two dragonflies flying around him. My mother had bought us the movie *Dragonfly* and we watched it often. We had believed after that dragonflies represent eternal life. Some may say it's a coincidence, but we know better. A few weeks later Jeremy was testing for his next belt in Jinjutsu when a dragonfly flew into the dojo and circled him before he was tested. He would have passed either way, but he did say it relaxed him.

When my father passed away we noticed the heavy presence of cardinals. My daughter Danielle it was a rabbit that reminded us of her memory. How deep or spiritual you want to take it or believe it is your business, but it's nice to place a certain object, animal, or song to continue to remind us of a loved one.

The all-star team fell short, but Jeremy gained some ground. August was a hard month; both my son Billy and I had birthdays in this month. His birthday was on the sixteenth, and as hard as you try to make it a special day, you can't help but to think of what is missing. When someone or something is gone, you feel the void.

My family kept the kids busy and upbeat right up until the first day of school that year. Billy was starting sixth grade, Jeremy was going into fourth, and Casey was in second grade. I thought this day was going to be tougher than usual because Agnes had always made their first days of school special. It was going all right until I dropped Jeremy off at school. He broke down and wanted to go to his mother's grave and say a prayer. Jeremy was a good student, so I was able to take him to pray and then let him stay home a few more days. Some might say I was just prolonging the inevitable, but I had faith in him and he continues to amaze me to this day. My three children all had different ways of dealing with their loss. Initially, there is nothing but pain. Then everyone's healing process is something no one can predict. Birthdays and holidays are givens, but certain days may mean more to some then others. The first day of school affected Jeremy more than Casey or Billy. Mother's Day seemed to have a deeper effect on Casey. These days might give you some indication of an issue or it might just appear out of nowhere. Be vigilant on yourself and your loved ones. Prepare yourself for certain days, maybe songs, or even certain places that might begin to break that mending heart.

We had received information from a few different people about group therapy for people who have lost a loved one. A lot of people around me suggested I take the children. So many people told me it couldn't hurt. I finally agreed, but I wasn't a big fan, so I guess I went in with a not-so-great attitude.

I don't know what the kid sessions were about, but the adult session was exactly what I thought it would be. The first two people talked about how they lost their loves ones, which was fine, I have no problem with that. Then we moved on to a woman who was there because she lost a dog. I still love the animals I've lost, but I can't see the purpose in those losses crippling my life for two years. A dog's life can't be compared to a human's. You may consider me cold for saying that, but I don't have time to mourn a dog. I've had a lot of dogs in my life, and, yes, I was sad when they died, but after a month you have to let them go.

Chapter 44

I have heard people say that the more you are exposed to a situation, the more you become immune to it. For example, people always say doctors can be cold when it comes to dealing with death because they see it so often. I know some police officers and firemen who say the same thing about being exposed to things time and again. Am I numb to these things? Of course not! I just put them into perspective.

People were great for a certain amount of time, but they can't help you forever, nor should you want them to. I guess it could be compared to a child's life. As parents, we would love to be there for every fall or let down, but we can't. No matter how involved you are in your children's lives, they will make choices on their own—both good and bad. I believe that I can only give my kids a good foundation; the rest is in their hands. My father used to say, "The older you get, and the smarter your father will seem."

A coach once told me, "You don't truly know how to win, unless you've lost before." That can be applied to life as well. In sports, when you lose a game, you sometimes have to change your approach to win the next one. If you suffer a loss in life, you most likely will have to change your approach to achieve your goals.

Change is going to happen, sometimes for the good and sometimes for the bad. Again we all heal at different physical and mental speeds, but if you set a goal you'll always have something to aim for. If one approach fails, try something else.

For me it has been, and continues to be, difficult trying to live up to the standards Agnes and I wanted to live by. Every time I think I've got something figured out, something new comes along and keeps me trying new things or approaching it from different angles to find the formula that works.

Anyone who says he has everything figured out is lying. Some days things go great, you have all the answers. Some days every move you make is wrong. My best advice is to roll with the punches and stay on your game. There are things to be learned from good days and bad.

At the time my in-laws were still living with us. It had its pros and cons, but it was just prolonging the inevitable. The whole family needed to expand their horizons and learn to take on new tasks. Change doesn't occur overnight, even now we're still trying to fill the void and figure things out. Have we been knocked back, knocked down? Sure we have. The important thing is we've gotten back up and looked for the right fit.

Here I am, a single father with three kids. Each child has his or her own paces and approach. It is important to show each of them every day that they are special.

I've tried to teach my children to channel negative thoughts into something positive. I've taught my boys to workout to counter the effects of stress.

I try to be more sensitive to my daughter. This is where I believe I'm not up to par. I know I can love her and be sensitive to her needs, but there are things that only a woman can teach a girl. Growing up with four sisters has helped. Between all her aunts and her grandmothers, Casey gets a lot of female attention, but she's with just the three of us boys most of the time.

As for me, I'm doing okay. There are times when I definitely feel cheated, but I was never the one who dueled on the why stage. On one particular gloomy night during that first Christmas without Agnes, I talked myself into some potato chips and sour cream. I know it wasn't the greatest choice at that time, but it I figure it's fine to indulge every once in a while. But, I never did get a chance to eat the chips that night because when I took the bowl out for the sour cream I placed it on the counter next to the mail. It was then that I noticed a letter with the donor's seal on it. I never wanted any of Agnes's organ recipients to feel as if they had any obligation to my family, so I never left any contact information. This letter was from a woman who worked for the donor organization. She wrote to me saying she respected my decision not to be contacted or to contact any one, but one of the families who had benefited from Agnes's organs felt compelled to write a letter. Inside the envelope was this man's story on how happy he was to have another holiday season with his father, how special their family's celebration was going to be. He also felt bad that we had to lose for their gain. He told me that our family was in his prayers. He promised that his family would never take their gift for granted.

Agnes may have been gone but she was still giving Christmas gifts. That letter put me back on the right track. I needed to stop thinking of what could have been and now move on to what would be. That man and his family were hopeful for a new opportunity and that's how I would be. It was Agnes herself that told me she was impressed with how I always demanded more of myself and never settled for less. This was no time for me to get discouraged. I had three kids who needed me. It would be how I handled things, how I faced adversity that they would learn and heal from.

About two weeks later I received another letter from a man who also received one of Agnes's organs. He had a wife and two daughters. He explained that he spent most of his life working and didn't get to spend all that much time with them. He told me he always wanted to provide for them and thought he would have been able to until he was told the bad news that he needed a transplant. He wrote about how months went by so fast and he was just relishing every moment he had to spend with his girls. Then he got the news of a donor, another chance. His outlook was different now, and he wanted to give them more than just a good life; he wanted to give them a piece of him.

I've saved the letters for the children to read when they are older, when they can truly understand how special their mother was.

I've experienced so much loss in my life, but I have never forgotten anyone I've lost. I live everyday to the fullest, regardless of what that day has to bring for me. Are there days when I want to just take a day to cry? There sure are. The funny thing is that when those days come, I can hear Agnes saying how I gave her the strength to look past the negative. When I do cry, I do it alone and when everything is quiet. When those times come, I let everything surface to get it out all at once.

I'm not sure this way works for everybody, but I know it works for me. I can handle that hit and recover quickly. My advice to you would be to ease yourself into it and see what you can and can't handle. If you dig deep within yourself, you'll find the strength you'll need to pull yourself up from any depth. Surround yourself with positive people, positive places to make it easier on you. Time will heal; it's just a matter of how long it takes.

Billy, my mother, Jeremy and Casey

Part 6

Mom

It was Mother's Day and calls to my mother were going to voice mail. My mother was living with my sister Maryanne and brother-in-law Pete. She had to give up her independence after she was diagnosed with cancer in late February. After calling for the fourth time, I called my sister to ask if she was taking a shower or maybe someone was visiting her. It was not much later that she was taken to the hospital because she fell on the stairwell. What we thought would be a short stay turned out to be much more. She had been given a year to live, however that time fame would prove to be way off. The year was now reduced to weeks, or maybe just days?

 The weeks leading up to my mother's death were very hard on me. This was the first time for me that death had become a matter of waiting. Everyone before this had gone quick, without suffering. I don't know if it's easier or harder. It was nice to have that time to say goodbye, however, it's at the cost of the person who is sick. Death is never easy. Just hard and harder is how I'd describe it. For a little more then a week, I don't think I felt more selfish. Each day I would leave the hospital praying for that one more day, one more hour, or even that one extra breath more. I would think of how irreplaceable she was. You just can't replace some people. It becomes a matter of you being able to adjust and adapt to something different. There's only some things you can prepare for and there are things left to deal with.

I remember sitting in the dark hospital room, holding my mother's hand as she slept. I was thinking of all the things I'd soon miss. Our time was limited but my memories were long. It's when we lose someone that we see how the little things add up. And yes, the little things are better than nothing. Mother taught me it's not so much about doing everything right, but it's about making things right. The room's silence had such loud conclusions. Time is the only war we can't win, but we could use every moment to our advantage, our joy. As I get older, I see that the true gifts in life are those things that don't fade, break, or tarnish.

My mother had a very humble upbringing. She was the oldest child and had a younger brother and sister. The family of five accomplished a lot with having so little. My grandfather Lunney had been in the navy, and was a World War II veteran. He was a no-nonsense type man, willing to do anything for anyone. He was also a big Red Sox fan. He seemed like the only Sox fan around, as everyone else liked the Yankees. But, he was also my biggest fan. He came to all my games and pointed out all the things he thought I did right, and told me to work on the things he thought I did wrong. He would tell me even Ted Williams made mistakes, but he worked really hard to make sure he didn't make mistakes as often. He was right because we all fail. Nobody is perfect. It's how we respond to our failures or loss that makes the difference. That's a lesson my grandfather taught me that never left me.

My Grandmother Lunney was my example of faith; there wasn't a day that went by that she didn't pray the rosary. She was the most unselfish person I knew. Whenever we ate dinner at her house, she made sure everyone was all set before she would sit down and eat. Back then it seemed like a common practice and I never paid much attention. But now, when I look back, I see how important a lesson it was. Thanks to Grandmother Lunney, I learned that you couldn't always put yourself first. You can gain a lot by making someone else smile. It was apparent that my mother learned so much from her parents.

You've seen my mother's name mentioned many times throughout this book. She stood by me through the good and bad. She did so much for my children after Agnes died. I consider myself blessed to have had such an influence in my life. Words can't completely describe her, but she led with her heart. Even when she got the bad news that her time was limited. She decided to focus on her kids and grandchildren. That speaks volumes about a person when they take on this type of roll. Although it was heartbreaking, I learned a lot about how courageous my mother was.

Looking back it seems my mother might have seen the writing on the wall, well before any doctor gave the diagnosis. I'm sure she had her moments of being scared, but she didn't show us. She took in everything around her with almost a new heightened appreciation of life.

Of all the things I learned from my mother, I didn't think courage would be one of them. I was wrong. She showed me how much fortitude she had. She always placed others first; she never thought about herself. All she wanted was to make peace with God and she was ready to accept whatever came next. The medical staff made a point to tell us how my mother would thank them after even the simplest procedures. What an example she was setting for all of us.

She exemplified making the most of the time, life, and functions that she had left. When she slept I could see how much pain she was truly in. but she hid it well behind her smile and laughter when she was awake. That was her way of taking as much stress off of us as possible. She even put it on herself to choose all her own funeral arrangements.

Forgiveness is another quality that reminds me of my mother. She was always ready to give someone another chance. In today's world, that could be considered a fault. It takes a big person to forgive and with that being said, it should make that person, who receives forgiveness, want to be a better person.

This next story is Christmas spirit at its finest. My mother wanted to buy a North Face jacket for my daughter for Christmas. She was walking around with the last size "small" in her hands when a woman approached her. The woman asked if she could just try it on because she was going to order one online and wanted to be sure of the size. Without hesitation, she handed the jacket over. The woman did try it on, and then proceeded to the register to buy it. I hope she got good use out of it. Some people will never change. It's all about them and will never pay it forward.

As forgiving as Mom was, she always found it difficult to forgive herself. Looking back, I guess people from her generation held themselves to a higher standard.

Forgiveness is an amazing quality as long as you do not allow yourself to be continually hurt by the same person or situation. You can't always blame yourself for the actions of others. Some people can't and or won't change. I guess it's true when they say you can't change everyone?

Chapter 45

As I've said throughout this book, love is the greatest thing we could offer or wish for. Love has no limits. As people we seem too complacent with love. We lose our appreciation of it. With different people we have different bonds, different degrees of love maybe. I've heard people say they "fell out of love" or that they "stopped loving." I don't think that is possible. I think we just allow our love to stop growing.

We are teaching the next generations that the growth of our bank accounts is more important than the growth of our hearts. As humans we only utilize a small fraction of our brains and now we are choosing to do the same with our hearts. Most underdogs are measured by the size of their hearts, more so than any of their other qualities. Movies are made of those who exhibit their hearts, yet we shelter it and harness it from its full potential.

In society today we are judged more on what we've done wrong than what we've done right. It's as if were trained to see the bad in someone. It just might be that we don't do as many acts of kindness anymore. It's been a year since my mother's passing, and again I am reminded how priceless memories are. Actions may speak louder than words, but words can hold their own. We all know words can wound, but they can also heal, help, and inspire. I guess it's all how we want to be remembered?

Chapter 46

I do once every so often think of what I had, and what I have lost, but that only strengthens my bond with what I have now. If you take any lesson from this book, I hope it is how to make the most of things. Make the most out of the opportunities you're passionate about. You may never get that second opportunity, so prepare yourself for when it does.

My parents Mary Ann and Bill Gannon

Mom with Casey

Part 7

Lessons I've Learned

While I certainly don't have all the answers, one thing I do know is that no matter how much time goes by or how many tears are shed, you can't change the past. If you have experienced a tragedy, lost someone you love, or done something that perhaps wasn't in your best interest or using your best judgment, learn from it and do better next time. It's true that time heals all wounds; with love those wounds heal a little faster. Love is the greatest thing on this Earth. It's the one thing I pray that my children will always have. Money, cars, and houses are nice, but they can't compare to a heart that's true.

I still have a few bad days every month. I have about a month's worth of really bad days in my entire life. A really bad month doesn't outweigh the really good years. Life truly is what you make it, so live it to its fullest.

I've been told that I'm strong, that I have strong shoulders. I suppose I do, but I've noticed that the stronger a person is, the greater the burden put upon him. Be careful what you wish for. At some time in all our lives, we will have to deal with pain, there's no getting around it.

Set your goals for you and your family. No one knows how long we have in this world, so make both long- and short-term goals. Agnes and I never got our chance to go to Hawaii, but we did accomplish everything in between. We shared a love that will last a lifetime.

So, do you still feel bad for me? Don't. I am a lucky man to have loved, be loved, and continue to love the way I do. Is that what makes me strong? I don't know, maybe. My heart has been broken many times, but I am not afraid to put it out there again.

From the day we're born, we're in a fight against time. The clock only moves in one direction—forward. We should follow suit and do the same as soon as possible. Whether it is finding a person or passion to move you beyond your past, find what it takes. Feeling bad is fine; living bad is a sin. Talk about it, write about it, or dream about it, then step past it.

I've never forgotten the pain, so I won't tell you to forget yours, but I do say learn from it and better yourself. I laugh at the days I thought were bad before the car accident. The day I lost my daughter was by far the worst day of my life, and I got through it. Every other day can only be better.

When bad things happen, people are going to talk. Whether the talk is good or bad, you better be prepared for it. There is no premium for privacy anymore; people don't know when to leave someone's business alone. Words can be powerful, especially when they move in a positive direction. I have had so many people influence or inspire me with their words. Words can also hurt. I think you have seen how I deal with negative words. I use them to my advantage by fueling my drive and proving that I am a better person for it.

People are mean. Kids can be cruel growing up, but adults are worse. With each generation we seem to be losing the values that our grandparents lived by and tried to instill in our parents. Respect has gone right out the window. The world has become a feeding frenzy on gossip. People need to remember that there are *always* three sides to a story: yours, mine, and the truth. It's like when you were a kid and your parents told you to look both ways before you crossed the street. Do that when you hear something about someone—look at both sides and decide when and if it's time to proceed, then proceed carefully.

My goal is to do something nice for someone every day. It could be getting someone a gift, giving a donation, or just talking someone through hard times. It's amazing how compassionate people can be when they try. Do we need a bad thing to happen to our hearts for us to see the need for compassion? People's hearts have hardened; most are quick to jump to conclusions just because you do something nice. They wonder why and think you have ulterior motives. Complements fall under the same category. It's no wonder people don't bother anymore. People need to learn to laugh again. We are the wardens of our own prisons. We are the only ones who can free ourselves. I could spend a lifetime dwelling on what went wrong and what I've lost, but that's not who I am. All those I lost are cheering me on and depending on me to be there for those we have left.

Like most parents, I struggle everyday on what is best for my children. For some reason, our society has lowered its standards to make people feel good about themselves. Everyone gets a trophy in Little League; everyone gets a ribbon at the local fair. What is this teaching our children? Competition is a good thing and a part of life. I couldn't imagine where we would be with out it. I can't speak for anyone else, but I know it feels a lot better to me if I accomplish something that no one expected I could. I read an article the other day about some people who were thinking about not having an All Star League so it wouldn't offend the kids who didn't make it. They already have back up teams for the kids on the line, and if